Praise for
8 Great Dates on true beauty, cool
from moms who have comp

"8 Great Dates has given me the tools I need to verbalize some very valuable lessons. I am grateful for this guide to help me along this journey with my daughter. I feel better equipped as a mother!"

Tracy

❀

"The…dates have provided a beautiful springboard through fun memories for me and my girls to communicate about growing up, finding identity in Christ, and how to biblically navigate through the tricky pre-teen years."

Melanie

❀

"My daughter and I…went on a date a month. We looked forward to each date and what we would do together. When my youngest daughter turned ten, she asked me when we were going to start going on our dates together!"

Tina

❀

"My girls and I love the dates. Love it!"

Wanda

❀

"After two years my daughters still remember and talk about what they learned…We are taking a 'refresher' course with the dates again this summer. A memory that will last a lifetime!"

Lynda

❀

"I just started using 8 Great Dates. We have done the tea party and the art museum date. I thought it was a perfect way to make the comparison of my daughter's beauty with fine art."

Sacheen

❀

"We have a lot of different interests and have just had some hard time 'bonding,' but when we discovered the 8 Great Dates book last year, that all changed. God began to work in our lives in such a way that all I can seem to do when I think about it is cry. Hands down, going on our dates has been the highlight of both of our lives over the past year!"

Jennifer

"We are having so much fun doing our own Secret Keeper Girls group using 8 Great Dates. We have had two group dates so far, including our tea and facial parties, and the girls can't wait for our next one. Thank you for preserving our daughters!"

Deb

✿

"We did the dates as a small group study of moms with their daughters!"

Shari

✿

"We are in the second year of doing Secret Keeper Girl as an outreach with a local home for children. We have another local church interested in doing the same."

Pat

✿

"I have one daughter, who is nine years old—almost ten. There are so many wonderful memories with her, and we are going through your Secret Keeper Girl Bible Study book and enjoying our dates immensely."

Joan

✿

"My daughter, Megan, and I enjoyed all of our dates as she learned what it meant to be a Secret Keeper Girl. My absolute favorite moment, though, was when my husband was able to join in on date night. Megan was beaming as she heard the praise from her papa about the amazing, godly young woman that she is becoming and the hope that lies ahead."

Wynne

✿

"I have so many wonderful memories with my daughter from this last year...thanks to you and your '8 great dates for you and your daughter' book. But by far, my best memory was the least 'jazzy' date. It was the one where we got away and spent some quiet time with God. When we got home, my eight-year-old daughter wrote this:

God has ben very good in my life but this time was
the best evrer becase I had a date with my very own mom
some pepole may think it's werd but i don't think that
mom and I had the best time ever and at the same time
we got more time with god wich was a blessing
nothing coud compair to that good date
i know that was short but i gotta run see ya.

Jennifer

8 great Dates for Moms and Daughters

How to Talk About True Beauty, Cool Fashion, and...Modesty!

DANNAH GRESH

HARVEST HOUSE PUBLISHERS
EUGENE, OREGON

Cover by www.DesignByJulia.com, Colorado

Interior photos of girls, moms, and dads by Steve Tressler, Mountainview Studios

Secret Keeper Girl is a registered trademark of Dannah Gresh

HARVEST KIDS is a registered trademark of The Hawkins Children's LLC. Harvest House Publishers, Inc., is the exclusive licensee of the federally registered trademark HARVEST KIDS.

8 GREAT DATES FOR MOMS AND DAUGHTERS
Copyright © 2003, 2010 by Dannah Gresh
Published by Harvest House Publishers
Eugene, Oregon 97408
www.harvesthousepublishers.com

Library of Congress Cataloging-in-Publication Data

Gresh, Dannah.
[Mother's planning guide for secret keeper girl]
8 great dates for moms and daughters / Dannah Gresh.
    p. cm.
Originally published: Mother's planning guide for secret keeper girl. Chicago : Moody Publishers, c2003.
ISBN 978-0-7369-6114-1 (pbk.)
ISBN 978-0-7369-6115-8 (eBook)
    1. Mothers and daughters—Religious aspects—Christianity. 2. Girls—Religious life. 3. Beauty, Personal. I. Title. II. Title: Eight great dates for moms and daughters.
BV4529.18.G74 2010
248.8'431—dc22
                                        2010009069

Printed in the United States of America

18 19 20 21 22 /VP-NI/ 10 9 8 7 6 5 4

To my mother, Kay Barker,
who told me the teacup story and taught me to live it.
Thank you for praying this verse over my life.

"Look…and be utterly amazed. For I am going to
do something in your days
that you would not believe,
even if you were told."
—Habakkuk 1:5

Acknowledgments

A Big SKG Squeeze to…

Over 140,000 moms and daughters who have been through these dates in the book Secret Keeper Girl: 8 Great Dates for You and Your Daughter, *where they first appeared.* I've loved getting to know my Secret Keeper Girls and their "connecting moms" through Facebook and my secretkeepergirl.com blog. I love you, girls! Thanks for getting Secret Keeper Girl rolling. We had no idea how big it would become!

Harvest House Publishers for partnering with us for the exciting growth of Secret Keeper Girl. I am so grateful that you see my heart to protect little girls in a culture that's pressing them to grow up way too fast. Thank you for re-releasing this, the original Secret Keeper Girl product, and for having the vision to encourage me to write *Six Ways to Keep the "Little" in Your Girl: Guiding Your Daughter from Her Tweens to Her Teens.* I'm especially grateful to Terry Glaspey for steering the partnership. Bob Hawkins Jr. and LaRae Weikert were especially generous with their time as we built the vision. Carolyn McCready invested no small amount of patience and expertise as a loving editor. Paul Gossard brought all the details together. I'm humbled to work with such veterans in the publishing industry!

Dr. James Dobson for recommending this, the original Secret Keeper Girl product, in your much-anticipated book Bringing Up Girls! Your encouragement means a great deal and will expand this message greatly!

While I'm at the task of squeezing, I'm so grateful for my main squeeze, Bob. Secret Keeper Girl was his idea, and he has been faithful. From our great beginning with Moody Publishers through Greg Thornton's leadership to our expanding our partnerships, Bob has married administrative genius with patience.

Mostly, thanks to Jesus, who I long to be with every day. I am forever in His Great Love.

—*Dannah*

Contents

Preface
9

Part 1
Getting to Know Each Other

Chapter One: A Mother's Seasons of Emotion
13

Chapter Two: Your Daughter's Endless Season
of Emotions: The Tween and Teen Years
17

Chapter Three: How to Use
8 Great Dates for Moms and Daughters
23

Part 2
8 Great Dates

Date Number One: Your Beauty in God's Eyes
33

Date Number Two: Real Physical Beauty
45

Date Number Three: The Source of Beauty
55

Date Number Four: The Power of Beauty
65

Date Number Five: Truth or Bare Fashion
75

Date Number Six: The Bod Squad
85

Date Number Seven: Internal Fashion
95

Date Number Eight: Affirmation of Beauty
105

PART 3
Devotions and Other Good Stuff

Secret Keeper Girl Devotions
115

Secret Keeper Girl FAQs
139

Notes
153

Girl Gab Pullouts
161

Hi, Friend—

In your hand is one of the easiest-to-use resources you'll ever find. Let me give you a few key pointers about how to find things in this book. (In just a few pages, I'll explain how to use it and how to plan your mom–daughter dates.) But here's a quick look at what you'll see inside.

Part 1: Getting to Know Each Other. This is a hearty "hello" and "welcome" to Secret Keeper Girl. The first two chapters contain some self-reflection on our own quest for true beauty and modesty as moms, and then a dose of truth about the culture your daughter is growing up in. Skim them if you want, but don't skip the third chapter. It tells you how to use the book!

Part 2: 8 Great Dates. Here they are in all their glory—the Secret Keeper Girl 8 Great Dates, which teach your daughter about true beauty and modesty! Glance through them and you'll see that each one is easy to use…and very fun. (What mom wouldn't want to share a facial with her daughter?)

Part 3: Devotions and Other Good Stuff. This section is full of things you'll reference as needed. Don't worry—I'll let you know when you need to dive in. The first part is the Secret Keeper Girl

Devotions. You'll use these fantastic daily devotions after Date #3, and I'll explain how to use them. The next section contains some frequently asked questions. I added this as moms wrote in with their most perplexing problems about true beauty and modesty. (I even tackled swimsuits!) Finally, you'll find the Girl Gab pull-outs for your daughter. These are identical to the Girl Gab pages you'll find in part 2—8 Great Dates. They're perforated so you can pull them out and give them to your daughter.

Enjoy!

Dannah

Part 1

Getting to Know Each Other

Chapter One

A Mother's Seasons of Emotion

Well, here you are.
A woman.
A mother.
How do you feel today?
Beautiful or boring?
Well-groomed or well-worn?
Are your kids ready to name you Nag of the Universe because it's "that time of the month"? Or is your husband ready to name ovulation a national holiday because it's that time of the month?

Are you feeling flabby and overweight? Or tan and toned?

Are your friendships building you up and giving you courage? Or have they left you raw and lonely?

Is your heart in a good place and filled with strength and confidence? Or are you carrying a wilted spirit?

Me?

My brain is mush today. I can count on these days, every month. There are three of them. I'm extra tired. I'm thirsty like I just ran a mile. (Believe me, it's been years!) I have a dull headache. To my husband and kids I *am* a dull headache!

I feel a little lonely. I'm weepy. And my brain…what was I just thinking…yes, pure mush!

But catch up with me in a few days—I'll be back on top of the game again. Energetic! Confident! Thinking a mile a minute even if I couldn't run one if my life depended on it. Enjoying my fabulous family.

Can you identify?

We women certainly are…well, I've heard it termed "emotionally wealthy"! I like to think of it as little seasons of emotional change.

Sometimes it's a mini-season like a day or two of a hormonal shower. Sometimes it's an extra-long winter that just won't warm up—brought on by the loss of a family member, the loss of a job, the rebellion of a child or the sickness of a spouse, the death of a dream, the judgment of a friend.

I had one of those long winters last year. Loneliness. Rejection. Numbness. Tears. A loss of direction.

During that long winter of growth my friend visited.

"What do you sense in me?" I asked, wondering if I was as bad off as I felt.

"A wilted spirit," she said, empathizing.

Tears flowed.

I felt pretty wilted.

She prayed specifically for God to water my soul. Funny thing—He did! The next morning I just happened to read Isaiah 55. (I'd been making my way through that particular book of the Bible.)

> *"Come, all you who are thirsty, come to the waters…As the rain and the snow come down from heaven, and do not return to it without watering the earth and making it bud and flourish, so that it yields seed for the sower and bread for the eater, so is my word that goes out from my mouth: It will not return to me empty, but will accomplish what I desire and achieve the purpose for which I sent it. You will go out in joy and be led forth in peace."*
> Isaiah 55:1,10-12

The watering began.

Three days later, as I completed my Bible-study homework, that beautiful passage was reintroduced to me with a new freshness…from God the author's perspective. "Come, all you who are thirsty, come to the waters."

I came.

The watering continued.

Oh, the fresh outpouring of God's Spirit during those seasons of emotions!

Can you identify? Have you found the fresh outpouring of His Spirit during those short mini-seasons like bad-hair days and PMS? Have you felt it overwhelm you like an ocean during those long winters of emotional pain?

Again and again, have you returned to the Word of God to find that it has the power and authority to arrest your unhealthy emotions and replace them with His truth about your value...your beauty...your purpose?

You may have picked up this cute little book with the intent of helping your daughter, but I'm praying that it would renew you and me too. That it would bring us back to the simplicity of soothing our emotions in Him as we train our sweet girls for the seasons ahead.

Won't you return to Him right now?

Bring the wilted parts of your heart to Jesus and ask Him to water them?

Just stop for a moment and ask the precious Holy Spirit to make you a well-watered place of refreshment before you go any further. After all, how can we bring that refreshment to our daughters if we've not first found it ourselves?

"Come, all you who are thirsty,
come to the waters."
Isaiah 55:1

Chapter Two

Your Daughter's Endless Season of Emotions: The Tween and Teen Years

V itamins and herbs.
  Lots of water.

A diet emphasizing whole grains and veggies and avoiding dairy and simple carbs.

The freedom to sleep a little more.

A commitment to bite my tongue.

A husband who promises to never ask, "Is it that time of the month?"

These things and a well-marked calendar pretty much get me through PMS!

Hormones!

Hopefully, you too have learned to identify the patterns of your emotional roller coaster and have found strategies to regulate them.

But did you have that maturity when you were blindsided by hormones at age 12? Do you remember the hopelessness that enveloped you when you woke up with your nose speckled with another outbreak of acne? Did you ever just fling yourself on your bed and lie there for hours, wondering if the world would even notice if you were gone? Did you ever completely avoid looking in a mirror altogether because it made you feel so bad? How about the day your friends didn't include you…again? Or the way you had a nervous stomach on the first day of school every single year, wondering if you'd know anyone in your classes?

Oh, my sweet new friend, our dear daughters are about to enter into a season of emotion that's been unknown to them. Their little bodies will soon be barraged with once-foreign chemicals. Their minds will be gripped by thoughts they still can't imagine thinking. The long winter of emotion will seem to last forever. They will have days, weeks, or even months when they feel as if they've been called to climb Mount Everest in the midst of a blizzard with no sign of a warm fire or cozy tent. The time to arm them with truth to make it through that season is now!

Dennis and Barbara Rainey liken the many perils of the teen years to a field full of bear traps—traps with grim, gray, steel-toothed jaws. They say,

Those traps, what about them? How much of a threat are they? We are convinced that far too many parents are lulled to sleep during the tranquil elementary years. Unaware of the approaching perils of adolescence and of how quickly they arrive.[1]

Our girls are as naive as we once were. And sometimes as mothers we fail to recognize just how many more traps are out there now and how much more quickly our girls fall into them.

For starters, girls are beginning to menstruate earlier. Most girls begin between the ages of 10 and 13, but some begin as early as 9. Now, what fourth-grader do you think deserves the hassle of pads before recess? Along with the pads you might also see this lovely list of new traits in your daughter:

- unpredictable emotional outbursts
- a quarrelsome spirit
- lack of self-confidence
- loss of interest in hobbies and tasks
- inability to concentrate (otherwise known as mush brain!)
- sensitivity to noise
- irritability, nervousness
- food binges

Body Image!

Of course, the food bingeing for you and me was kind of like, "Hey, pass the chocolate!" followed by giggles. Today, food binges aren't to be taken lightly, as they can start a terribly disruptive spiral into bulimia or anorexia. We cannot be naive and think that our daughters won't fall prey. They are constantly being fed a lie of what a beautiful body looks like. The average model today weighs 23 percent less than the average woman today. When you and I were teens, the average model was only 8 percent thinner than the average woman.[2] A recent Harvard study showed that two-thirds of underweight 12-year-old girls thought they were fat.[3]

Anorexia and Tweens

Bulimia—bingeing and purging—commonly starts during the high school or college years and affects about 4 percent of all young women. But especially watch out for anorexia—excessive dieting and denying the body of food. It often targets the brightest girls…the highest achievers…in their early adolescent years. It affects only about 1 percent of young women, but once it has made itself at home, it's among the most difficult emotional disorders to treat and has the highest fatality rate! See anred.com for more information.

Boy-Craziness!

Hormones and body-image lies aren't the only traps for our sweet girls. Boy-craziness hits during the pre-teen years, if not the early elementary years. It may not hit your daughter, but it's certain to hit her circle of friends. Some parents chuckle passively at this "cute" little trend. Let me let you in on a secret. Being in a dating relationship for six months or longer is a significant risk factor for teen sex. Since a girl's primary sexual organ is really her heart, the longer she stays in a relationship, the more she lets her guard down. Can you see how this "cute" little boy-craziness can be a set-up for serial dating, which places her heart and body at risk?

Many of these issues and other high-risk activities in tween and teen young women can be traced to a preoccupation with their body image and sense of beauty. A bad-hair day or a broken nail can become an obsession. Some girls will spend more time in front of the mirror than in their schoolbooks. Tiny flaws will begin to rule their mind. Women, we simply must rise up to speak truth to our daughters!

Fashion!

And of course, we can't talk about the truth of their bodies without hitting the subject of fashion. Belly rings. Miniskirts. Bare midriffs. Tween girls are now wearing thongs! (And not the kind that go on your feet.) When I blogged about this at secretkeepergirl.com, I was disheartened to find some moms (though few) defending it. (This despite—besides the question of modesty—the concern from the medical field that thong underwear increases the risk of infection.)

I'm mad!

But I'm also hopeful.

Look at the fabulous women who made an impact on our world during their own tumultuous season of teen emotions.

Joan of Arc.

Anne Frank.

Rachel Scott.

Mary, the mother of our Lord Jesus Christ.

And without a doubt each of these was climbing Mount Everest in a blizzard! I believe with all my heart that the primary reason Satan sets so many traps for our precious teens is that he knows how much power and potential for good they can unleash in our world.

We should not underestimate what our daughters can do. Instead, we should encourage them to be an example to believers in conduct, in faith, and in purity.

We can stay mad, or we can get smart.

Let's intelligently and lovingly arm our daughters with truth for the season ahead. *8 Great Dates for Moms and Daughters* focuses on your daughter's image of her body and how she'll choose to present it in the years to come. It will not only help you teach your daughter the truth about her beauty and what God thinks about fashion, but it will also teach her the art of soothing her emotions with the refreshment of the Spirit of God.

And you'll both enjoy a strategically timed batch of fresh, hot brownies along the way!

"Don't let anyone look down on you because you are young, but set an example for the believers in speech, in life, in love, in faith and in purity."
1 Timothy 4:12

How to Use "8 Great Dates for Moms and Daughters"

When I wrote the first edition of this mother–daughter interaction guide in 2003, the word *tween* wasn't very common yet. But I had one. She was ten years old, and her name was Lexi.

I knew when Lexi fell asleep at night. Her mouth finally stopped moving. She'd been like that since birth.

Sometimes out of sheer self-preservation, I would tune out. That little beauty was on to my game. Every now and then, just as I was about to immerse myself in an imaginary bath of Calgon, I'd hear her little voice bursting the bubble of my fantasy.

"Mom, what did I just say?" she'd challenge.

I know I'm not alone here. At some of my events I ask the teen girls what they most want to change about the way their moms communicate. Nearly every time a hand will raise and a freckle-faced, braces-laden beauty will say, "Like, she sometimes isn't very focused when she talks to me. If she could, like, just not wash the dishes or totally stop taking out the trash when I'm talking and, like, well, really, totally look me in the eyes and, like, listen!"

Right about then I start feeling, like, really totally guilty!

How to Be a "Connecting Mom"

One of the greatest factors in reducing high-risk teen behaviors such as early sexual activity, violence, and substance abuse is parent–child connectedness. (Translated: "like, well, really, totally looking our kids in the eyes and, like, listening!") I've written an entire book for you just about how to become a "connecting mom." It's called *Six Ways to Keep the "Little" in Your Girl: Guiding Your Daughter from Her Tweens to Her Teens,* and it'd be a great companion book as you do these 8 Great Dates together.

My dream for the original *Secret Keeper Girl: 8 Great Dates* was that it would be a tool to help moms spend focused time connecting to their little girls. It's become that, and so much more. Over 140,000 moms and daughters have done these 8 dates since the book came out in 2003. As a result, my team and I are poised on the front lines to protect the heart of tween girls as the culture insists they grow up...too fast!

And Secret Keeper Girl has taken on a life of its own, with our central focus being the Secret Keeper Girl Tour, a live event that provides the most fun a mother and daughter will ever have digging in to God's Word. We've added fiction books, a Bible study, and another 8 Great Dates kit about true friendship. And we've initiated The Modesty Project, a collection of moms who want to be a positive voice for the retail and fashion industry, which sometimes needs to be reminded that we want to buy modest and age-appropriate clothes for our little girls. (Check out the whole world of Secret Keeper Girl at secretkeepergirl.com.)

What You'll Find in This Book

8 Great Dates for Moms and Daughters is fun-filled interactive "dates" for you and your daughter to explore God's truth about true beauty and modesty. Each date is about one-and-a-half hours long (excluding your planning and travel time during the date). Be sure to take a camera along for at least some of the dates so you can have photos for the Secret Keeper Girl scrapbook you can create as an optional activity! (More on that later.) You can do these dates weekly or just spread them out and do them as you can schedule them into your life. Just don't let them get too far apart. While each date will have a different topic and activities and even a slightly different order of events, they will all have the same features. Your date from start to finish will include the following:

SKG Prep Talk

The Prep Talk gives you a little challenge of your own and an overview of the date. It's best if you plan to read through this section a minimum of *several* days in advance. That way you have time to make appointments or reservations or schedule special guests into the date.

SKG Radio: 7–10 Minutes

There's one really cool aspect to these 8 Great Dates that requires a touch of technical skill. (You can recruit someone to help if you are technically challenged. You'll only need help once.) Visit secretkeepergirl.com and download the free audio MP3's that accompany these dates. After you download them, you can either burn a CD for the CD player in your car, or just store them on your iPod or MP3 player so you can play them for your daughter on the way to and from the dates. These SKG radio moments really support your dates. I'll be right there "with" you to share a story and get your hearts moving in the right direction for your upcoming activities. Can you get by without them? Probably, but they really do add a lot of depth to your experience. Go ahead. Tackle technology!

SKG Girl Gab: 15–25 Minutes (with optional scrapbooking afterward)

You'll need one fun and funky scrapbook for your daughter, if you want to do this in the ultimate way. A simple 99-cent spiral-bound book will work, or you can go all out and visit a place like Michaels for something with bells and whistles. (If you really dislike scrapbooking, you can skip that altogether. The important part is that you do the Girl Gab pullout pages.) The main purpose of the scrapbook will be to store your Girl Gab pullouts after you've filled in the blanks on your date. Later on, you can also add photos of the dates and other memorabilia like tickets or receipts. Don't do your fun scrapbooking as a part of your date time. Stick to the simple task of filling out your Girl Gab pages supplied at the back of this book.

SKG Challenge: 30–45 Minutes

This is the real fun! The challenge is what you'll do at your special destination. (Think facials, tea parties, and shopping!) These are either object lessons or simply fun activities for you and your daughter that will give you great opportunities to share with your sweet girl!

Here's an overview of the fun
in store for the two of you:

Date #1:

Your Beauty in God's Eyes

Challenge activity: A tea party

Key verse: Isaiah 64:8

Key thought: A Secret Keeper Girl is God's masterpiece.

Suggested challenge setting: A tearoom

Date #2:

Real Physical Beauty

Challenge activity: A facial or manicure

Key verse: Song of Songs 6:8-9

Key thought: Real physical beauty is the
unique qualities that only I have.

Suggested challenge setting: A full-service
spa or the home of a facial consultant

Date #3:

The Source of Beauty

Challenge activity: A quiet encounter with God

Key verse: 1 Peter 3:3-4

Key thought: The source of my beauty
is the presence of God.

Suggested challenge setting: Any place of solitude,
such as a quiet mountain, a sunset beach, a
cabin, or even a candlelit bubble bath

Date #4:

The Power of Beauty

Challenge activity: A study of art

Key verse: Proverbs 5:18-19

Key thought: The intoxicating power
of beauty is my responsibility.

Suggested challenge setting: An art gallery

Date #5:

Truth or Bare Fashion

Challenge activity: Shopping with Mom in a vintage store

Key verse: Philippians 2:14-15

Key thought: I must express my beauty carefully.

Suggested challenge setting: A vintage clothing store

Date #6:

The Bod Squad

Challenge activity: Shopping with friends

Key verse: Proverbs 13:20

Key thought: My expression of beauty is
strongly influenced by friends.

Suggested challenge setting: A local mall
or a favorite department store

Special needs: You'll need one to four of your daughter's
friends and their moms for this one. Preferably they'll
be also doing Secret Keeper Girl Dates or will at
least hold to the same values that SKG teaches.

Date #7:

Internal Fashion

Challenge activity: A new haircut or special updo
Key verse: 1 Corinthians 11:8-10
Key thought: My beauty is ultimately
determined by what I wear on the inside.
Suggested challenge setting: Professional salon

Date #8:

Affirmation of Beauty

Challenge activity: A dress-up date with
Dad (and Mom!) to affirm your daughter's beauty
Key verse: Psalm 139:13-16
Key thought: God calls me a princess.
Suggested challenge setting: An upscale restaurant
Special needs: Dad (or a grandpa or big brother)

Budget Crunchers

If money is a big concern, relax. In the few lessons that may be more expensive, I'll offer you tips on how to do it economically. Keep in mind that this option may require more time and planning.

Small-Group Alternative

This needs to be fun, and in the area of modesty/fashion, it's really important to build a positive peer pressure among the girls in your church, school, or community. Date #6 requires you to have one to four of your daughter's friends and their mothers participate. It's far more effective if these girls and women have been learning the same things you've been studying during your dates. Therefore, you might encourage these mother–daughter pairs to do the 8 Great Dates along with you. You'll still "do" most of the book alone with your daughter, but you'll have two or three mothers taking their daughters through it at basically the same pace so you're all ready to do date #6 at the same time. (It might be fun for the moms to meet for lunch now and then to update and encourage one another. We moms need all the encouragement we can get!)

SKG Radio: 3 Minutes

On your way home, just flip your CD or MP3 player back on for a special surprise. Former recording artist and bestselling author Rebecca St. James and others will share some of their own secret moments of struggling with beauty and fashion. To find out who you get to hear from, be sure to visit secretkeepergirl.com as soon as you can!

SKG Driveway Prayer: 3–5 Minutes

You'll wrap up each great beauty date with an intimate prayer in your driveway. Don't skip this vital time of growing closer through the power of God's presence. Your book will give you an idea of what you might pray, but feel free to go in whatever direction God leads you for this time.

Well, that's pretty much it.

Ready to start planning your first date?

Part 2

8 Great Dates

Your Beauty in God's Eyes

Challenge activity:
A tea party

Key verse: Isaiah 64:8

Key thought: A Secret Keeper Girl is God's masterpiece.

Suggested challenge setting: A tearoom

SKG Prep Talk

School photos can be unkind.

Just weeks before my sixth-grade photo, I'd emerged from the beauty salon with my first real hairstyle. After two visits, the stylist had finally relented and cut my waist-length sunshine-colored tresses. I left with shoulder-length "feathers" to rival Farrah Fawcett's. I loved it.

By the time of my seventh-grade photo, I'd emerged smack dab in the middle of puberty. My sunshine-blonde, full-bodied hair had become a dishwater-blonde, oil-laden cap. In one year I'd gone from having fantastic feathers to being an ugly duckling.

And I have it all frozen in time thanks to the school photographer.

My mother became my lifeline of truth. She never told me that my hair wasn't darker or that my hair and skin weren't oilier or my body wasn't thicker. She just made it okay with her well-timed and not overfocused affirmation. She assured me that God was just returning to His masterpiece to do a little more work.

Dannah in sixth grade.

Dannah in seventh grade.

Prep Talk with God

Take a moment to pray. Pray that God would help you pour out heartfelt affirmation upon your precious daughter. Lift each part of her beauty and body up to the Lord. Start at her head and work all the way down to her toes!

Planning Date #1

Value-Evaluation Tea Party

Subject: Your beauty and value in God's eyes

Setting Options: A tearoom, special restaurant, or bed-and-breakfast

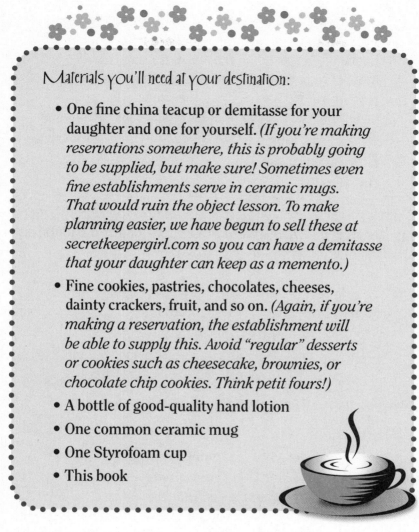

Materials you'll need at your destination:

- One fine china teacup or demitasse for your daughter and one for yourself. *(If you're making reservations somewhere, this is probably going to be supplied, but make sure! Sometimes even fine establishments serve in ceramic mugs. That would ruin the object lesson. To make planning easier, we have begun to sell these at secretkeepergirl.com so you can have a demitasse that your daughter can keep as a memento.)*

- Fine cookies, pastries, chocolates, cheeses, dainty crackers, fruit, and so on. *(Again, if you're making a reservation, the establishment will be able to supply this. Avoid "regular" desserts or cookies such as cheesecake, brownies, or chocolate chip cookies. Think petit fours!)*

- A bottle of good-quality hand lotion

- One common ceramic mug

- One Styrofoam cup

- This book

I want you to thoroughly pamper your daughter during this date. Find an exclusive little teahouse or a swank hotel and make reservations for an extravagant tea. When you call for reservations, explain what you are planning and ask these questions:

A. "Can you serve the tea in fine china or porcelain?" (Make sure they can serve you on beautiful porcelain or fine china, not ceramic or bone china. If you can't find a place with the right stuff, either purchase some that can be given as a gift at the end of the date, or borrow some of your great-grandma's china. The hotel or restaurant will work with you if they know what you are up to, and if you can come at a less busy time of the day. An afternoon tea would be just perfect.)

B. "Can you serve dainty desserts? What would my options be?"

After you've scheduled your location, read through the rest of the date so you're prepared to present the object lesson during the challenge.

**SKG Radio
7–10
Minutes**

Play "Date #1: Your Beauty in God's Eyes" as you drive to your destination.

There are three stages to your challenge:

**SKG
Challenge
30–45
Minutes**

1. Hand massage

Upon arrival, let your daughter enjoy the environment, and if you don't have a predetermined menu, go ahead and order. But then your very first act of pampering will be to give her a hand massage. Get down on your knees and lovingly use that fabulously scented hand lotion you brought to give your daughter a great massage.

2. Tea party

You may end your massage about the time that the tea arrives or shortly thereafter. Then, just enjoy the yummy food and fellowship together.

3. Object lesson

Now, it's time for you to make this all have meaning. I've prepared a brief object-lesson script on the next page. One quick read-through should prepare you.

. . . .

Where to Go for Tea

Not sure exactly what kind of place you're looking for? Here are a few specific ideas.

❀ *A special hotel*

In Hershey, Pennsylvania, the hometown of Hershey chocolate, there is a nearly antique, immaculately kept establishment called the Hershey Hotel. It has a glass-walled restaurant that overlooks gardens. And the desserts are far from ordinary! A special hotel near you may be just the place.

❀ *A local bed-and-breakfast*

Some bed-and-breakfasts specialize in custom lunches and teas as well as overnight stays. My husband, Bob, and I once stayed in one in Helena, Arkansas, which had a breakfast so lavish that he got confused about what went with what and poured the gourmet chocolate sauce on his eggs. To find a bed-and-breakfast near you visit www.bedandbreakfast.com.

❀ *A "chick-food" restaurant*

A dear friend once took me to a place near Virginia Beach, Virginia, called The Painted Lady. This lavishly painted Victorian gingerbread home featured dainty little finger foods, salads and soups, and a live pianist. Many towns have little restaurants like this, which would be just perfect.

You may live in Texas or Canada or Australia, but you get the idea! You're looking for a place to be uniquely pampered. Ask around and make a few phone calls.

. . . .

Object-Lesson Script

Mom: This is really special, isn't it! If you could describe in one word how you feel right now, what would that word be?

Daughter's response: (Hopefully she'll say something like "pampered," "special," or "loved.")

Mom: What if I had just taken you to the local restaurant and bought you some tea in this cup? (Bring out the regular ceramic mug.) Would you feel as special?

Daughter's response: (Usually a girl will say no.)

Mom: What if I'd just stopped at an old diner and gotten you some tea to go in *this* cup? (Bring out the Styrofoam cup.) What would you do with this cup when you were finished?

Daughter's response: (Usually she will say she'd throw it away.)

Mom: But tonight (or today) we've been served on fine china and (describe the other special circumstances of your date, such as "with dainty pastries, and the tables are covered in white linen and..."). These three cups can tell us a lot about our value. Like Dannah (pronounced like "Hannah") said on our tape, you are incredibly valued in God's eyes. That's why He takes so much time to work with you, just as a potter with his clay. Your value doesn't change...ever...but the world will often judge your value based on how you present yourself. In the eyes of those around us, we're either throwaway Styrofoam cups, everyday old ceramic mugs, or priceless china teacups in the way we dress, talk, or act, or in the places we're willing to go. Do you ever see girls presenting themselves as "trashable" in any of these ways? (The ways we dress, talk, or act, or the places we're willing to go.)

Daughter's response: (Could vary. She may name a specific friend or stay with general trends. Be prepared to simply direct the conversation for a few minutes. Let her express her thoughts about what you've just said.)

Mom: Well, I know I'd rather be a precious piece of china, but sometimes I need to be reminded of where I'm falling short. So, tonight I'm going to let you evaluate me and I'm going to evaluate you.

This will be the first time you present your daughter with her new scrapbook (if you're planning to do that). You might want to gift-wrap it or put it in a fun bag with a special pen, along with her first page from Girl Gab, which you'll find at the end of the book. All you need to do is pull them out and prepare to use them. Your own Girl Gab page is right here.

During each Girl Gab time, you'll let your daughter read the introduction, and then both of you will just discuss and do the page together. It's all about getting her to gab her heart out so you can hear what's in it! For this date, you'll ask her to fill out her Value Evaluation. Give her about five to ten minutes to do this and then use the rest of your time to discuss the evaluation.

Your daughter's "Girl Gab" for this date begins on page 161.

Budget Cruncher

If cost is a concern, just get out your best linens and china (borrow them if you need to) and buy some dainty cookies. It would be best to go away from home to a special place. Ask a friend or relative who has a beautiful home or a lovely porch if you can set up there. Or find a babbling brook and set up a table and chairs nearby. Keep service simple so you can just spend time with your daughter.

Welcome to SKG. That stands for *Secret Keeper Girl*. What is a Secret Keeper Girl? Think hard and you may remember. Can you fill in this blank?

_____

A Secret Keeper Girl is one who keeps the deepest secrets of her beauty for her future husband. Also, she knows that there aren't any secrets she can't share within the safety of her relationship with her mom. And the coolest thing about a Secret Keeper Girl is that she is a masterpiece created by God.

> *"We are the clay, you are the potter; we*
> *are all the work of your hand."*
> Isaiah 64:8

God Himself took the time to carefully craft you into being! You must be a masterpiece!

Value Evaluation

Okay, let's take girl talk to a new level. It's called Girl Gab. So, are you a Styrofoam cup, a ceramic mug, or a priceless piece of china in the following areas? Look over the list and then write an X in the column that best fits you.

	Styrofoam	Ceramic	China
In the way I talk about my dad or husband			
In the way I talk to my mom or daughter			
In the clothes I wear			
In the clothes I want to wear			
In the way I care for and style my hair			
In the way I care for my face each day			
In the way I care for my body and skin			
In the time I spend with God each day			
In the way I treat other people			
In the movies and TV I watch			
In the magazines I read			
The friends I select tend to be…			
My friends tend to pull me toward…			

Now for each area where you selected "Styrofoam" or "Ceramic" for yourself, come up with one specific idea of how you can move toward presenting yourself as a priceless piece of china.

Areas Where I Need to Improve the Way I Present Myself

Okay, how can you improve? If you gave yourself a "Styrofoam" evaluation for the way you've been watching TV, think of something you need to do to change. You might write, "I'm going to try to watch only 30 minutes a day, and only after my homework is done."

Areas Where I Need to Improve

1. . . . .
. . . .
. . . .
. . . .
. . . .

2. . . . .
. . . .
. . . .
. . . .
. . . .

3. . . . .
. . . .
. . . .
. . . .
. . . .

4. ....
....
....
....
....

5. ....
....
....
....
....

Take some time as mother and daughter to encourage each other in those areas where you want to improve.

SKG Radio
3 Minutes

Play your audio files as you go home. Find out what surprise Christian recording artist will be there to encourage you!

SKG Driveway Prayer
3–5 Minutes

As you arrive home, spend a few minutes alone in the car praying for each other in such a way that you affirm each other as a masterpiece of God.

Real Physical Beauty

Challenge activity:
A facial or manicure

Key verse: Song of Songs 6:8-9

Key thought: **Real physical beauty is the unique qualities that only I have.**

Suggested challenge settings: **A full-service spa or the home of a facial consultant**

SKG Prep Talk

Certainly this wasn't happening.

Not yet.

But I could see it with my own eyes.

Physically, I saw a lanky nine-year-old girl pulling her little body up onto the bathroom counter so she could lean close to the mirror. Her eyes scanned the reflection, studying...no, scrutinizing...until they sighted a victim—a slightly crooked tooth. She began to push at that little tooth with her tiny fingers. Her eyes squinted, as if loudly speaking her criticism of this imperfection.

Spiritually, I saw a precious daughter of Christ entering for the first time into a battle she'd face again and again and again.

I wanted to run into that bathroom and set the physical world in order—to tell Lexi we'd fix it and would call the orthodontist for an appointment that very day. Instead, I stood outside the door and called upon God to set the spiritual world in order in one little girl's heart.

Prep Talk with God

Won't you take a moment right now to present your daughter to the King of kings? Ask Him to stake a claim at the doorway to her eyes—so all she sees when she looks in the mirror would be that which He desires her to see.

Planning Date #2

Studying My Own Beauty

Subject: Real physical beauty

Setting Options: A full-service spa or the home of a facial consultant

Materials you'll need at your destination:

- A couple of beauty magazines, such as *Teen Vogue* or *Seventeen* (optional: See information in the SKG Radio section to follow)

- Items you need for the facials (the spa or specialist should supply everything)

- This book

This date is really about getting in front of the mirror and identifying both your and your daughter's unique beauty strengths… from head to toe. You'll do this by getting her (and yourself) in front of a mirror for a special, pampering facial. Learning the discipline of skin care before problems begin can delay or avoid them altogether.

Select your destination. No matter whom you use, try to spend some time on the phone with the person who will actually be giving the treatment to your daughter. Tell her the purpose is twofold:

1. to encourage your daughter in the unique aspects of her beauty
2. to train her to take care of her skin

Read over the rest of the date ahead of time so you can be prepared or so you can prepare your salon specialist to go over the areas in the challenge.

SKG Radio
7–10 Minutes

Play "Date #2: Real Physical Beauty" as you drive to your destination.

Note: As an option for this date, you may want to purchase a magazine or two that portrays an unrealistic view of beauty, such as Seventeen, YM, *or* Teen Vogue. *It would be a good tool for viewing as you both listen to the audio. Also, on the following page you'll find a link to some interesting true beauty images, videos, or both that I update to keep current. I will not mention that these are available in case you'd prefer not to share them with your daughter.*

Budget Cruncher

The Mary Kay option should alleviate most budget concerns for this date. However, keep in mind that you can always prepare your own spa at home, which might be great fun! Simply show up in bath slippers and housecoats, cover the same information as above, and use these yummy recipes.

❀ Body-cleansing cucumber water

Lots of spas are beginning to serve cucumber water, as it is an antioxidant for the body. Even if you're having an in-home Mary Kay facial, this drink could be a fun addition to your spa night.

   1 seedless cucumber, thinly sliced
   1 pitcher of water with ice

Soak the cucumbers in the pitcher of water for a few hours before you serve it. This releases the cucumber juice into the water. Serve in fun glasses with one cucumber slice on top!

Makes 4 to 6 glasses.

❀ Peach facial

   1 medium peach
   1 tablespoon of warm
      honey-cooked oatmeal

Cook the peach until soft and then mash it with a fork. Add warm honey and enough oatmeal to make it a thick consistency. Apply to the skin while it's still warm! Add a few cool cucumber slices to the eye area. Soak in the yummy aroma for ten minutes, then rinse with cool water.

Makes enough for 1 to 2 girls.

(Of course, don't use this if your daughter has allergies to any of the products in it.)

Do the following during your daughter's facial:

1. Call her attention to specific and unique beauty strengths.

This is simply a compliment or two such as "You have very creamy, white skin. It reminds me of Snow White!" or "Your eyes are definitely show stoppers. They're so bright and blue I think I could swim in them!"

2. Teach her how to cleanse her skin carefully.

If you're working with a professional, you won't need to help with this part. If you're doing it at home, here are some pointers. She should learn to

a. cleanse her face at least once daily

b. use warm (not hot) water and her hands or a soft washcloth

c. touch the sensitive areas around her eyes very gently

d. avoid touching her face excessively during the rest of the day

3. Emphasize that makeup is not necessary to enhance her beauty at this age.

In the year 2000, the Medical Institute for Sexual Health

Cover Shot Beauty Unmasked

In 2004 the makers of Dove products unleashed the "Campaign for Real Beauty." Women the age of most Secret Keeper Girl moms were photographed without regard to size, color, wrinkles, or other natural beauty marks. I liked it. In fact, we wanted to use their Evolution of Beauty video at our Secret Keeper Girl live events, but couldn't get permission. So we created our own. Stop by our website to see my twentysomething friend Jen Wilton taken from natural beauty to unrealistic perfection with the use of lights, makeup, and electronic touch-ups. It's a great way to show your daughter that beauty isn't always what it seems!

Find it at secretkeepergirl.com!

identified the top five factors that place a teen girl at risk for sexual sin.[4] One of them is "appearing older than she actually is." On the other hand, girls who "appeared to be their actual age" tended to be less at risk.[5] How does a girl appear older than she actually is? By the way she wears her hair and presents her face as well as by the clothes that she wears. Lip gloss—and in some extreme cases, corrective base makeup—is okay, but overall makeup can wait! Having your professional skin expert say this will carry a lot of weight, and if you buy your daughter some special lip gloss to top the date off, it'll let her know it doesn't mean she can't have fun.

SKG Girl Gab
15–25
Minutes

When I use this curriculum in a small-group setting, I'm always surprised to find that girls as young as eight or nine are worried about their weight, height, hair, underdeveloped breasts, over-developed breast buds, big feet, large nose, crooked teeth, or freckled skin! They're not too young for a serious talk about body image.

This date's Girl Gab time allows you to find areas where your daughter may lack confidence and need some extra encouragement

Specific Ideas for Skin Care Date

There are two directions you could go for an effective facial date. Either one will be special.

A local day spa

Look in your Yellow Pages or ask around for advice. Call the spa and explain what you are doing. Some spas only accept clients of a certain age. You'll need to verify that both you and your daughter can be serviced.

about her body image. It's vital that this encouragement come from you. Studies show that when mothers criticize their daughters' weight or appearance, it increases the risk of eating disorders.[6]

As your daughter points out a weakness or insecurity, your job is to truthfully state a word of encouragement. Here are some encouraging but truthful responses to criticisms.

> *"Oh, honey, that crooked tooth is getting straighter and straighter every day as your mouth grows and makes room for it. And I think it's kind of cute!"* (I've used that one myself!)

> *"I didn't realize you felt self-conscious about having breast buds. It's really a very exciting thing. Let's celebrate by going bra hunting this weekend!"* (Then, of course, do it!)

> *"You're right, your skin is becoming a little more sensitive, but maybe that's God's way of keeping you well-grounded. Just think how absolutely perfect you'd be if it weren't for that one tiny flaw!"* (My mom used that one on me more than once!)

Your daughter's "Girl Gab" for this date is on page 165.

A Mary Kay consultant

If you go to www.marykay.com or check local listings, you ought to be able to find a Mary Kay consultant in your area. Lots of moms and daughters who have completed these 8 Great Dates have used one to host a simple and fun date of learning. The consultant will give you advice free of charge, but it's only kind to spend a little bit with her on some products. Consider giving your daughter $10 to $15 to buy some lip gloss or skin-care products. (And treat yourself to something too!)

Date #2: Real Physical Beauty

Girl Gab

So, Secret Keeper Girl, can you find God's definition of beauty? Dig deep down under all this world's junk and you'll see it. It's nothing like what we imagined it might be. God's Word says this:

> *"Sixty queens there may be and eight*
> *concubines and virgins beyond number;*
> *but my dove, my perfect one, is unique."*
> *Song of Songs 6:8-9*

Real physical beauty is those special things about you that are unlike anyone else. Kind of funny, isn't it? Those are sometimes the things that make us feel most uncomfortable because they're...well, different. But God says that's what makes us beautiful. I want you to look at yourself piece by piece today. Can you see that unique beauty?

My Unique Beauty

Complete the sentences below. Then, talk about it as mom and daughter.

My hair is_____

My eyes are _____

My nose is _____

My teeth are_____

My face is_____

My complexion is _____

My smile is _____

My weight is _____

My height is_____

My chest is_____

My legs are _____

My hands are _____

The most unique physical trait about me is _____

Okay, let's be real. We all have things about us that make us feel more bashful than beautiful. What's yours?

. . . .

. . . .

. . . .

Guess what? God has got that covered! Second Corinthians 1:4 says,

> *"Praise be to the God of all comfort who comforts*
> *us in all our troubles so we can comfort others!"*

Some people might try to tell you that braces or zits are no big deal. But they are! Anything that makes you feel bad is a big deal. Just don't forget that God wants to comfort you. And He just might use you to help the dozens of other friends around you who feel the exact same way about the exact same thing!

SKG Radio
3 Minutes

Play your SKG audio for the ride home. A surprise Christian recording artist will share her beauty secrets.

SKG Driveway
Prayer
3–5 Minutes

Spend a few minutes alone in the car praying for each other. Later today, ask the Lord to affirm your daughter in the unique aspects of her beauty and ask Him to pour confidence into the areas where she said she feels insecure.

The Source of Beauty

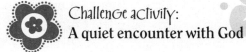

Challenge activity:
A quiet encounter with God

Key verse: 1 Peter 3:3-4

Key thought: The source of my beauty is the presence of God.

Suggested challenge setting: Any place of solitude, such as a quiet mountain, a beach at sunset, a cabin, or even a candlelit bubble bath

SKG Prep Talk

I was 26.

And my life was, well, messy. Mediocre and fruitless at best.

Oh, from the outside it looked pretty neat and clean. Picture-perfect, really. A cute little house with a yard that had won "Yard of the Month." A husband who was well-known in our little community. A son. A daughter. A nice brick church to call my own.

So, why wasn't I even remotely happy? Why was I yearning for something?

Behind the façade, my house was cold. My marriage was shallow on its best days and filled with anger on its worst. My kids were confused. My career was exhausting. I was depressed. My church was an unfulfilling social outlet.

Then one day, at the end of my rope, I picked up a book that challenged me to spend one hour a day with God. Part of me laughed. How would I squeeze that into my day? Stay up until two in the morning? But I was desperate.

After years and years of a petty 15-minute-a-day devotional life, I entered into a daily one-hour scheduled appointment with God. I remember sitting there the first day wondering if the hour would ever end, but after only four weeks of never missing that appointment, I felt myself changing.

My life was changing!

It was amazing, but the things they say about Christ actually changing someone…I was starting to believe them.

It was happening to me!

That was more than 15 years ago. I'm not quite as much of a stickler about spending one hour a day with God as I was then. Some days I'm engulfed in a much longer time of sweet communion with my Lord. Other days it's shorter. Starting it out as a specific (and longer than I was used to!) time commitment was what built the passion and habit and enabled me to begin to truly hear God's voice. I've been radically changed by this investment of my time.

My life today is a fantastic adventure. My home is warm. My marriage is passionate. My children are directed and happy. My career is more than I could have dreamed of. I am emotionally strong (excepting a season here and there that God uses to make me even stronger!). And I'm learning that the church is not a place I go. Rather, it is being Christ to those in need around me.

How about you? Is your life what you dreamed of? Or do you long for the purpose and adventure God created you to know? You will only find that place abiding in God's presence, my friend. John 15:5 says, "I am the vine; you are the branches. If a man remains in me and I in him, he will bear much fruit; apart from me you can do nothing."

There's nothing gray about that. You are either spending time with God and bearing supernatural fruit. Or you're doing nothing, all the while running frantically like a caged hamster on a wheel.

You need the refreshment of God to feel purpose. To bear fruit in your daughter's life. To be content.

Have you found that place? Are you abiding in Him?

Prep Talk with God

Please pause right now and ask God's Holy Spirit to guide you as you prepare this date. If spending time alone with God has been a struggle for you, confess that and ask Him to fill you with hunger to do it. Pray for your daughter to develop an intimate, ongoing conversation with God.

Planning Date #3

The Absolute Beauty Challenge

Subject: **The source of beauty**

Setting Options: **Any place of solitude such as a quiet mountain, a beach at sunset, a cabin, or even a candle-lit bubble bath**

Materials you'll need at your destination:

- **Depends on the location you select**
- **This book**

Lexi and I got to do these Secret Keeper Girl dates when she was 11. When she was 16, she told me that this had been her favorite date. Imagine that! The quiet encounter with God was the one she remembered the most. We went away to Stone Valley, a local state park, and rented canoes. After a little bit of fun on the water, we spent our time with God on a secluded "island" in the middle. I hope your quiet encounter with God is as memorable.

To get started, select your site. If weather permits, do it outside somewhere.

After you've selected your site and collected the items you need, determine if you will need extra time for this date. If you are taking a trail ride or a long mountain hike, you may need to plan for a longer time.

Read through the SKG Challenge and SKG Girl Gab to get yourself prepared to lead your daughter through this neat time with God.

Where to Find Solitude

❀ A mountain picnic

If you live near a hill or mountain that's known for its beauty, hike to an awesome view or find a babbling brook somewhere on it. Enjoy a light lunch or snack as you soak in the smells, sounds, and view. *Items needed: Hiking shoes, water bottles, backpack for picnic food and books, blankets to sit on.*

❀ A trail ride

Nearly every girl loves horses. If you and your daughter can ride, find a place to take a private trail ride. The key is that it must be private and you need to be able to stop and tie up the horses for your Girl Gab. *Items needed: Long pants, water bottles, backpack for your books, blankets to sit on.*

Play "Date #3: The Source of Beauty" from your SKG audio.

Note: Have this book handy so you can show your daughter this photo of me and my girls during the "true beauty confession" found on this audio message.

This date is unique. The SKG Challenge will be actually having a quiet communion with God in your special place. You need to do the Girl Gab *first* to set up the challenge. In most cases, you'll do Girl Gab right out in the special setting you've

🌸 A snow date

Want to do something really dramatic? There's nothing like the hush at night after a fresh snowfall. If you hit this date in the winter, tell your daughter in advance that it will take place on the next snowfall. When it comes, drop everything to just go sit in a quiet moonlit field of snow. You have to, of course, find a warmer place during your Girl Gab. *Items needed: Snow pants and coats, a thermos of hot chocolate, flashlights.*

🌸 A sunrise or sunset on the beach

Nothing is more heavenly than the beach at sunrise or sunset. When most people have gone and the sand alone is a rhythmic drum for the beating ocean, it's so easy to worship there. *Items needed: Bucket to explore and collect things, water bottles, a blanket to sit on, backpack for your books.*

chosen. But if you're doing a snow challenge or a bubble bath, you'll need to do the Girl Gab before you head out, in order to lay the foundation for the challenge.

Your daughter's "Girl Gab" for this date is on page 169.

Date #3: The Source of Beauty
Girl Gab

Where does beauty really come from? As girls we sometimes get stuck on thinking it comes from a great haircut or a totally awesome new fingernail polish. Sometimes we think it comes from being surrounded by beautiful friends or being noticed by cute guys. But these are dry streams. You won't find beauty there.

> *"Your beauty should not come from outward*
> *adornment, such as braided hair and the wearing of*
> *gold jewelry and clothes. Instead, it should be that of*
> *your inner self, the unfading beauty of a gentle and*
> *quiet spirit, which is of great worth in God's sight."*
> *1 Peter 3:3-4*

The source of true beauty is the presence of God!

The Absolute Beauty Challenge

How 1 Peter 3:3-4 is really challenging us could be said like this: "Do you spend more time in front of the mirror making yourself externally beautiful, or do you spend more time developing your inner beauty through quiet communion with God?"

I'd like to ask you to take my Absolute Beauty Challenge (A-B-C). Here's how it works:

A. Challenge yourself each day to spend a little more time with God than you spend working on your external self. If your morning beauty routine is 30 minutes, try for 40 minutes of time alone with God. Although I don't want you to get caught up in watching the clock, I know that pushing yourself in this area of discipline will change you immensely. Maybe your daughter takes about 15 minutes to get ready each morning—help her to set a goal of spending 15 or 20 minutes a day with God. I want you to do this for the next four weeks, for five out of seven days each week. And to make it really fun, put something on the line in case you miss a day. For example, you might say that if you miss, you'll clean your daughter's hamster cage the next week. If she misses, she might have to clean your shoe closet!

B. Agree to the challenge by signing the Absolute Beauty Challenge. When you get home, tape it to your bathroom mirror.

C. Every day, before you officially start your day, read the verse on the challenge and ask yourself the question, "Today, did I spend more time in God's Word or in front of this mirror?"

Are you ready to dive in? If so, sign the Absolute Beauty Challenge. Post it in your bedroom or bathroom where you can see it every day when you're getting ready.

Absolute Beauty Challenge

(It's as easy as A-B-C.)

*"Your beauty should not come from outward adornment,
such as braided hair and the wearing of gold jewelry
and clothes. Instead, it should be that of your inner self,
the unfading beauty of a gentle and quiet spirit
which is of great worth in God's sight."*
1 Peter 3:3-4

"Today, did I spend more time in God's Word or in front of the mirror?"

We, _____ and _____, will attempt to spend _____ and _____ minutes a day in quiet prayer and Bible reading during the next four weeks. We commit to doing this for five out of every seven days. If one of us misses more than two days in a week, that person will _____ for the other.

(Ideas of things you can do for each other if you miss more than two days include cleaning out the other person's closet, giving them a foot rub and manicure, walking the dog when it's their turn, or doing the dishes while the other one relaxes!)

Signed: _____

Date: _____

To make it easier to have devotions, *8 Great Dates for Moms and Daughters* includes 20 mini-devotions. See part 3 of the book.

After you've completed the Girl Gab, it's time to actually spend some time with God. Give each other just a little space and have your first quiet time then and there. Invite your daughter to turn to the first devotion in part 3 and do it.

Listen to one of today's Christian recording artists as she encourages you with some cool truth about her quiet time with God. Just listen in on the audio recording.

As you arrive home, spend a few minutes alone in the car praying for each other. Ask the Lord to speak to you powerfully in your devotional time over the course of the next four weeks and to help you maintain your commitment.

The Power of Beauty

 Challenge activity:
A study of art

Key verse: **Proverbs 5:18-19**

Key thought: **Guarding the intoxicating power of beauty is my responsibility.**

Suggested challenge setting: **An art gallery**

SKG Prep Talk

He glances at the curve of your body.

He studies the soft skin of your back.

He reaches for you.

A cascade of chemicals rush through his body like electricity flooding a dark stadium with light.

His mind is engulfed in adrenaline, blinding his judgment.

His touch becomes stronger. More demanding.

His body stiffens.

Your body senses his excitement and begins to soften.

The sweet intoxication has begun...and you are still fully dressed.

Don't blush! You have a daughter, my friend. At some point in your life you've experienced the power that your body has to intoxicate a man…to bring specific and thrilling changes in him. In the context of our marriages, this is a holy act of praise to our Creator as much as an act of passion.

But that cycle of excitement began with a glance. And all too often today's young women are indiscriminately offering young men and older men the chance to study their youthful curves and much of their tender skin. The cycle commences.

A godly young man will fight it for all he's worth.

But even many of them will fail.

Prep Talk with God

Have you ever taken time to consider and understand the beautiful way God created men to be intoxicated by their wives' bodies? Do you understand how our society is abusing that splendid power? Take time to ask the Lord to help you present this amazing responsibility to your daughter.

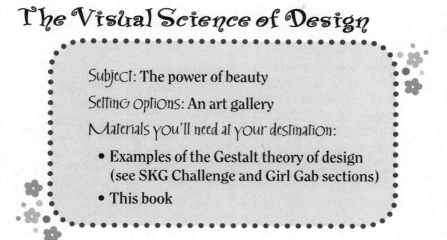

Planning Date #4

The Visual Science of Design

Subject: The power of beauty

Setting Options: An art gallery

Materials you'll need at your destination:

- **Examples of the Gestalt theory of design (see SKG Challenge and Girl Gab sections)**
- **This book**

This date will begin to establish the foundation upon which we can build the value of modesty. But we can't go there without talking about sexuality.

"Hold on there!" you might be saying. "I didn't bargain for that in this study." Well, let me give you a little dose of confidence. There are two reasons we need to go there now, while our daughters are between the ages of 8 and 12. First, for the most part our daughters haven't broken out into full, curvy womanhood just yet. Addressing this now alleviates the confusion your daughter could feel if you wait to talk about modesty after she develops. You don't want her to ever feel as if those beautiful God-given curves are bad. They're not! They're His masterpiece. Addressing the issue now separates the two so she gets the correct message loud and clear. Her body isn't bad, but some ways of dressing are.

The second reason to talk to her about it now is because modesty is, in fact, a vital part of her sexual value system. Don't take my word for it. I bet you've heard of at least a few of these credible leaders:

Josh McDowell states, *"Sex education at home must begin at a very young age and continue as the child grows up...If you wait for the 'big talk,' it will probably come too late. By the time you get around to it, your child will probably already know more than you do (or at least he or she will think so)."*[7]

Tim and Beverly LaHaye say, *"By age ten most girls and some boys have learned from their friends about...intercourse... Wise parents will share this information briefly, by the eighth or ninth year, to ensure that their child is accurately informed."*[8]

Barbara and Dennis Rainey challenge, *"We are going to assume that by the time your child is eleven or twelve, you have already shared some of the basic information about sex and human reproduction. If you have not yet begun discussing this topic, now is the time."*[9]

Dr. James Dobson states that *"you should plan to end your formal instructional program about the time your...daughter enters puberty."*[10]

We're not going to talk specifically about sex, but we will allude to the sexual attraction. After all, isn't that why we're teaching them to dress modestly?

For your date tonight, you'll select an art gallery or a museum to visit.

SKG Radio
7–10 Minutes

Play "Date #4: The Power of Beauty" from your SKG audio files as you drive to your destination.

You'll need to do your Girl Gab as a foundation for today's tour of art. Do this either in your car or inside the art gallery lobby.

SKG Girl Gab
15–25 Minutes

Your daughter's "Girl Gab" for this date is on page 173.

SKG Challenge
30–45 Minutes

Now, it's time to take a look at some art. Your quest is to find and identify the Gestalt-theory effect in as many places as possible. The Gestalt theory teaches an artist to control a viewer's time and attention by forcing the person to mentally complete a visual image. Because the brain is intrigued by completing the incomplete, it will always pause to finish an unfinished picture.

But don't simply run through the art gallery to locate examples. Stop at each piece and look it over, savor it, learn from it, and talk about it. Talk to your daughter about what it says about women and beauty. Stand in front of each piece and ask her questions like the following:

A. What does this say about feminine beauty?

B. Is this a healthy view of women?

C. How does this time period portray women differently from how we portray women today?

D. (If you are able to see art from different cultures): How does this society portray women differently from the way ours does today?

Once you've begun to make your way through the art gallery, I want to encourage you to explain in an age-appropriate manner exactly what Proverbs 5:18-19 means when it says a man is "captivated" by a woman's beauty. (The literal Hebrew translation would read, "May you be ever intoxicated by her sensuality.") There's no need to be terribly specific, and if your daughter is only eight or nine you may *consider* skipping this brief discussion. But please skip it only after you've spent some time in prayer asking the Lord if He wants you to do that. I believe we must begin to give our girls a true understanding of the mantle of responsibility that lies on their shoulders because of their power to intoxicate.

I've found that explaining the body's autonomic nervous system (ANS) really helps girls begin to understand the minds of men...without robbing them of their innocence. Here's a sample script for you to review.

Art Gallery Alternatives

The best scenario for this date is to find an art gallery, no matter how small. If you simply can't find one, try these alternatives.

🌸 Library

Some libraries not only have magnificent books depicting classic art, but they also have works of art within the library. If you don't research in advance what books you can look at, then plan on taking the time during your library visit to find some great art in books.

🌸 Bookstore

A large bookstore will have an art section for you to browse. Some will even have a coffee bar for you to sit in. Again, check it out in advance or leave a little time to explore and discover where the great art photos are hidden.

Script: The Power to Intoxicate

Mom: Do you remember what Dannah [pronounced like "Hannah"] said our beauty has the power to do to a man?

Daughter: (Some will remember the word *intoxicate,* and others may need help.)

Mom: That's right! Is a person in control when he's intoxicated?

Daughter: (Some will understand what this means, and some will need some help. Explain that it means to be out of control. If they've ever been anesthetized for surgery or dental work, you may use that to give them an idea of how a person might feel out of control. Or you can refer to the story on the audio about drunkenness. Be sure to remind them that everyone is responsible to make good choices, but in these situations, it is simply harder to do so.)

Mom: Well, when a man views a woman's body…whether it's her curves or some of her skin…he is intoxicated. I want you to really understand this, and I think I have a way that will help you. Do you remember ever being lost in the grocery store or the mall?

Daughter: (Let her share a specific time that she recalls.)

Mom: Well, do you remember how your body responded?

Daughter: (Answers will vary. Maybe she remembers her heart racing or her body sweating or a hot flash that swept over her. Help her along in recalling that feeling.)

Mother: Do you remember how long it took for that feeling to come over you?

Daughter: (It was probably immediate!)

Mother: That was your body's autonomic nervous system (ANS) at work. It's the part of your body that is created to respond to what it sees, feels, smells, and senses. You did not choose to have your heart race or your body sweat, but the ANS did this as a signal to you that fear was appropriate. This same system controls the attraction between a man and a woman. For men, there are very clear physical changes that take place in their bodies, just like the changes that took place when you felt lost.

A man isn't meant to experience those physical changes in his body with anyone other than his wife. But here's the difficult thing. Just like you didn't choose to have those changes in your body when you were afraid, a man doesn't necessarily mentally choose to become intoxicated. He can become intoxicated by what he sees around him.

And I want you to understand that this is how God created us. Who created our bodies to have that power?

Daughter: (God.)

Mom: Who created men's bodies to respond to that power by being intoxicated?

Daughter: (God.)

Mom: So the response is God's plan, but did you notice that the verse Dannah shared with us said, "Rejoice in *the* wife of your youth"? How many wives?

Daughter: One.

Mom: So the man is supposed to be intoxicated by only *one* woman. So how many men do you think God wants you to be intoxicating to?

Daughter: One.

Mom: A woman's belly. A young teen's bra strap. A beautiful woman in a really tight shirt. These things can all trigger a man's "intoxication" response. So, can you see how important it can be to dress in such a way as to honor the way God created men? Based on what we've learned about the Gestalt theory, do you think that sometimes the way a girl dresses could intoxicate a man even though she doesn't realize it?

Daughter: Yes.

Mom: What are some examples of today's popular fashion statements that you think might make a man's mind "finish the picture"?

Daughter: (She might come up with some things like low-riders, belly shirts, belly rings, miniskirts, short shorts, bikinis, backless shirts, or others.)

Mom: There are a lot of things that might do that today, aren't there? That's why I want you to be careful about the way you dress. It's why I try to be careful. I want to save the deepest secrets of my beauty to intoxicate just your dad (or, if you're a single mom, my future husband if God would want me to marry sometime). I want you to save the deepest secrets of your beauty to intoxicate just your future husband. Does that make sense to you?

Spend some time answering any questions she may have about this and helping her to find some examples of the Gestalt-theory effect in the art museum. Or look for it on billboards and bus ads on the way home!

God created your beauty with a special power. The Bible calls it the power to intoxicate. But it's for just one man…your future husband. Remember, a Secret Keeper Girl is one who saves the deepest secrets of her beauty for just one man. Each and every day the clothes you choose to wear are a part of saving the deepest secrets of your beauty for just him!

> *"May your fountain be blessed and may you rejoice*
> *in the wife of your youth. A loving doe, a graceful*
> *deer…May you ever be captivated by her love."*
> *Proverbs 5:18-19*

God created you with an intoxicating power called beauty, and it is your responsibility to handle it with care.

On the way home, play your SKG audio clip featuring a surprise Christian recording artist.

As you arrive home, spend a few minutes alone in the car praying for each other. Ask the Lord to help your daughter to understand the power of her beauty and to desire to save the deepest secrets of that beauty for one man…her future husband.

A Doodling Lesson

Check out this little graphic.

What do you see? You probably see a man.

Is he happy or sad? You might even guess that he's happy.

Hmm! I show you a couple of curved lines and a circle, and you see a happy little guy! What is up with that? That's the Gestalt theory at work. The Gestalt theory teaches an artist to control a viewer's time and attention by forcing the person to mentally complete a visual image. Because the brain is intrigued by completing the incomplete, it will always pause to finish an unfinished picture.

Check out this trio of circles.

What else do you see? (Answer: A triangle)

Can you draw a bird using the Gestalt theory? How about a mountain?

I'm not just telling you this for no reason. It has a lot to do with the power of your beauty. How? Well, what does a guy see when a girl walks by him wearing a tiny little pair of low-rider shorts and a belly shirt? Write your answer below:

. . . .
. . . .
. . . .

How about when a girl wears a long, tight skirt with a slit all the way up the sides?

. . . .
. . . .
. . . .

Are there any clothes you wear that invite someone to finish the picture?

. . . .
. . . .
. . . .

What can you do to avoid wearing clothes that invite people to finish the picture of your body?

. . . .
. . . .
. . . .

Your drawings here!

Truth or Bare Fashion

 Challenge activity:
Shopping with Mom

Key verse: Philippians 2:14-15

Key thought: I must express my beauty carefully.

Suggested challenge setting: A vintage clothing store

SKG Prep Talk

Here I was—34. Feeling 14.

When I'd purchased this outfit earlier in the day, it had seemed perfect. The lime-green T-shirt and linen overalls just "felt" like the beach. And the color really made me look tan! I couldn't wait to wear them, so I didn't. It seemed like a good choice. Until I got to this popular Southern California restaurant. Every other woman was dressed to kill.

A brunette walked in wearing tight leather pants and a white spaghetti-strapped tank.

A beach blonde sauntered in still wearing her dark sunglasses. Her miniskirt showed off her tan all the way to her slim thighs.

A woman ten years my senior strutted by looking far sexier than me in her simple tattered white shorts, silky blouse, and high heels.

So, here I was looking at myself in the bathroom mirror of this California hot spot.

I felt like a big green blob!

Prep Talk with God

Ask God to help you to be in touch with how it feels to be dressing differently than everyone else. Intercede for your daughter in this area—that she could have the confidence to do that very thing if she needs to, and understand why she's doing it.

Planning Date #5

Truth or Bare

Subject: **The practical application of modesty**

Materials you'll need at your destination:

- **Money to buy one outfit (optional)**
- **This book**

It's not easy dressing modestly. And it's a lie to tell your daughter that she'll never feel left out. She may feel less attractive than those who dress in clothes that reveal beauty's precious secrets. And in fact, in dressing modestly she may turn fewer heads than those who dress revealingly, even if she is lovelier. We need to…

A. tell her it's not only okay but a glory to God to not have to follow every fashion trend

B. creatively show her what fashionable modesty looks like

There are many sweet Christian teen girls who say they want to dress modestly, but their hearts and minds are so infiltrated by the world's billboards and their friends' immodest choices that they compromise. Our daughters need to see modesty in action, and they need some practical ways to test the clothes they choose to see if they are modest. For this date, you'll be having a hilarious look at fashion trends in a vintage clothing store. Then you'll be evaluating trends based on God's Word.

All you have to do to prepare is find the biggest and best vintage or secondhand store within driving range. Then read the rest of the date to get it into your mind.

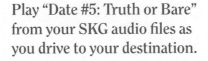

SKG Radio
7–10 Minutes

Play "Date #5: Truth or Bare" from your SKG audio files as you drive to your destination.

SKG Challenge
30–45 Minutes

For the challenge portion, find as many different "looks" as you can and try them on. You should each try on four complete outfits, including belts, hats, shoes, and any other crazy thing that might be on hand. The catch is that each outfit has to be a different "look." You might be the polyester queen in a pantsuit from the 1970s for one outfit. For another, go for the '50s flared skirt and cardigan. (Don't forget the Keds and bobby socks.) This may be easier for you than for your daughter, given that polyester suits weren't in style when she was five—so don't worry about sizes. Let her float in a ruffled bridesmaid dress from the '80s! The object is simply to have fun and observe how silly fashion trends can be.

If you find something you both like, buy it! Why not? It'll probably be a great deal.

After you've left the vintage clothing store, find a fun place to sit to complete the Girl Gab portion of your date.

Your daughter's "Girl Gab" for this date is on page 175.

Date #5: Truth or Bare Fashion

Girl Gab

In the '80s, when I was a teen, socks were huge! We had three pairs of socks to match each outfit, and we wore them all at the same time! We even had something called leg warmers, which were huge, fuzzy socks to wear over our jeans all the way up to our knees! Trends come. Trends go. Does God care about them? Fashion trends are not His biggest concern, but I think He does care. He certainly doesn't want us to just follow the crowd!

"Do everything without complaining or arguing so that you may become blameless and pure, children of God without fault in a crooked and depraved generation, in which you shine like stars in the universe."
Philippians 2:14-15

God's Word doesn't diss fashion. But it calls us to be careful in the way we express our beauty. If we obey Him, we'll probably stand out a little. That's a good thing. But we're always called to share our beauty cautiously!

Today's Hot Looks!

Okay, let's test all the current fashion trends against God's Word. First, read all the different fashion trends I've listed in the left column on the next page. Go ahead and add any that you think I've missed. Include specific things you've had your eye on, like a certain style of shirt or a pair of sneakers.

Now in the column labeled "How I see them," write down the main characteristics or things people wear when they're trying to get that look.

Today's hot looks	How I see them	Pass, fail, or use caution
The beach look	Suit, cover-ups, bikini	Bikinis fail. Use caution with a cover-up.
The prom look		
Miniskirts		
The cowgirl look		
Grunge		
Goth		
Preppy		
Punk		
Athletic		
The '50s look		
Designer labels		
Belly rings		
Tattoos		

Now you can decide if these looks *pass, fail,* or deserve *caution* based on a few Bible verses I think help us evaluate fashion. (Some of these will be familiar to you.)

Is this look feminine?

> *"A woman must not wear men's clothing, nor*
> *a man wear women's clothing, for the LORD*
> *your God detests anyone who does this."*
> *Deuteronomy 22:5*

God wants you to look like a girl...not a guy. That doesn't mean you can't wear pants. It just means you shouldn't wear pants that are cut for men or anything else that is considered manly in our society. Are there any things above that you feel God wouldn't want you to wear because they don't let you look like a girl?

Does this look hide my "intoxicating" secrets?

> *"Rejoice in the wife of your youth. A loving doe, a graceful*
> *deer...May you ever be captivated by her love."*
> *Proverbs 5:18-19*

God wants you to save the deepest secrets of your beauty... your breasts, your belly skin, your thighs, and your bottom...for just one man. Does this trend make you look fabulous without drawing attention to these parts of your body?

Is this look joyful?

> *"Be joyful always."*
> *1 Thessalonians 5:16*

God wants you to look like a girl who worships Him. Since worshipping Him fills us with joy, we need to make sure we don't clothe ourselves in dark and dreary attire. Are there any looks in the chart above that you should avoid for that reason?

Is it affordable?

"Your beauty should not come from outward adornment,
such as braided hair and the wearing of gold jewelry
and fine clothes. Instead, it should be that of your
inner self, the unfading beauty of a gentle and quiet
spirit, which is of great worth in God's sight."
1 Peter 3:3-4

God doesn't want you to be consumed with how much you spent on an outfit or whether it's a certain brand. It doesn't mean we can't have a certain brand if it's comfortable and affordable, but we shouldn't whine for things we can't afford. Are there any things in the chart that need to be disqualified for this reason?

Does it honor my parents?

> *"Honor your father and your mother, so*
> *that you may live long in the land."*
> Exodus 20:12

A Secret Keeper Girl can't wear anything her parents don't want her to wear, and she has to obey their preferences with honor. So, do you need to cross anything off for this reason?

Do I really like it, or do I just think my friends will like it?

> *"Am I now trying to win the approval of men,*
> *or of God?...If I were still trying to please*
> *men, I would not be a servant of Christ."*
> Galatians 1:10

It's okay to want something because you think it's neat, but watch out when you start buying things just because your friends have them.

SKG Radio
3 Minutes

Tune in to your SKG audio file to hear your surprise artist for this date!

SKG Driveway Prayer
3–5 Minutes

Take time to pray about your hearts...both of you. Is there anywhere you've compromised in the kinds of clothes you wear? Ask the Lord to give your daughter a willing heart to stand out like a star in the universe!

The Bod Squad

Challenge Activity:
Shopping with friends

Key verse: **Proverbs 13:20**

Key thought: **My expression of beauty is strongly influenced by my friends.**

Suggested challenge setting: **A local mall or a favorite department store**

Special needs: **You'll need one to four of your daughter's friends and their moms for this date. Preferably they'll be also doing SKG or will at least hold to the same values as SKG teaches.**

SKG Prep Talk

You like Ann Taylor Loft. She likes Justice.
You think "comfort." She thinks "cool."
You wear Merrell's. She wears Skechers.

As much as we'd like to remain the sole influencers in our daughters' lives, that just isn't going to happen...especially in the area of fashion. In a survey conducted for *World* magazine, peer pressure was named by female college students as a primary reason they chose the clothes they wear. Our daughters care about what their friends think. The best thing you and I can do is to guide them to select friends whose parents are establishing the same values that we're working toward.

Prep Talk with God

Pray as you prepare this date that your daughter and her friends would choose to influence each other positively in all areas of their lives. Pray for her closest friends by name.

Planning Date #6

The Bod Squad

Subject: Peer pressure

Setting Options: A mall or a department store

Materials you'll need at your destination:
Cash in the amount of $20 to $100

- Photocopies of the Truth or Bare Fashion Tests for all the moms (pages 89–91)
- Photocopies of the Girl Gab pages for each mother–daughter pair
- This book

Your daughter and a few of her friends will be learning through the SKG Truth or Bare Fashion Tests. These tests help her creatively determine if an outfit is modest or not. Start planning the date by determining who you'll be shopping with. If you know of other mothers who are doing SKG with their daughters, you've already got your shopping buddies. If not, you need to begin your planning by selecting one or two of your daughter's friends who seem to dress in the way you want your daughter to dress. Contact their mothers and explain what you are doing, and get the moms a copy of the Truth or Bare Fashion Tests to look at ahead of time.

Next, get your brains together to decide how much money you want to invest in the night. I suggest no less than $20, else they won't have enough to buy anything significant—and no more than $100, else the challenge will take too long. Each mother needs to feel comfortable with what you decide, and each girl needs to have the same amount of money to spend.

Select a mall or department store your daughters love. Here's my warning: Be prepared to bomb at some stores. When we shop using these tests, we sometimes have to completely redirect ourselves, especially during the summer months.

Select a meeting place and a time. You'll want to listen to the CD together, so if you can all fit into one vehicle, that'd be great!

Note to moms: Most of these tests aren't relevant to the majority of eight- to twelve-year-olds, so you may be wondering what the point is. Just as we prepare our daughters ahead of time for menstruation, we must also prepare them ahead of time for how to handle breast development and curves. Even if some of your daughter's outfits are okay now, when do you tell her she can't wear them anymore? When she's feeling totally awkward because her breasts are just budding, or when she's fully round and has been intoxicating many young boys?

I think it's better to prepare her now, in a fun setting with friends, and to let her see her developing womanhood as a joyous thing and not a nuisance that "limits" the fun things she can wear. And notice that we're also giving her the freedom to hold you accountable, so she is less likely to feel that this is an unfair burden you're placing on her.

SKG Radio 7–10 Minutes

Play "Date #6: The Bod Squad" from your SKG audio files as you drive to your destination.

You'll do Girl Gab as a group, so make copies of the pullout for the other girls who join you. As you arrive at the SKG Truth or Bare Fashion Tests, ask the girls to try them. If any of them is wearing an outfit that fails, don't back off from

SKG Girl Gab 15–25 Minutes

the validity of the test, but be kind as you speak the truth in love. Suggest a solution. For example, "Wow. Jennifer, it can be shocking to find out that a shirt you never even thought about might be a little low-cut. But you have great taste, and I really like that shirt. Don't get rid of it. Try to find a cool T-shirt to put under it."

Your daughter's "Girl Gab" for this date is on page 181.

Date #6: The Bod Squad

Girl Gab

Well, here you are with your special friends, otherwise known as The Bod Squad! Friends can offer good peer pressure to help you make modest choices in the years ahead. Remember, peer pressure is when your friends or acquaintances influence you to do what is right or what is wrong. Do you remember what I said about peer pressure and fashion on the CD?

> *"He who walks with the wise grows wise."*
> Proverbs 13:20

For today, it might as well read, "She who shops with wise friends will wear great fashion!"

Truth or Bare Fashion Tests!

Before we set you loose to shop, I have a few modesty tests every single outfit has to pass. I like to call them the SKG Truth or Bare Fashion Tests. Review each test and take them as a group.

Test: Raise & Praise

Target question: **Am I showing too much belly?**

Action: **Stand straight up and pretend you are going for it in worship. Extend your arms in the air to God. Is this exposing a lot of belly? Bellies are very intoxicating, and we need to save that intoxication for our husband!**

Remedy: **Go to the guys' department and buy a simple ribbed T-shirt (otherwise known as a Secret Keeper Girl Secret Weapon) to wear under your funky short T's or with your trendy low-riders. Layers are also a great solution to belly shirts.**

Test: Grandpa's Mirror

TarGet question: **How short is too short?**

Action: **Get in front of a full-length mirror. If you're in shorts, sit crisscross applesauce. If you're in a skirt,**

sit in a chair with your legs crossed. Now, what do you see in that mirror? Okay, pretend it's your grandpa! If you see undies, or lots of thigh, your shorts or skirt is too short.

ReMedy: **Buy longer shorts and skirts!**

Test: I See London, I See France

TarGet question: **Can you see my underpants?**

Action: **Bend over and touch your knees. Have a friend look right at your bottom. Can she see the outline of your underpants or the seams in them? How about the color of them? Can she see your underwear itself because your pants are so low that you're risking a "plumber" exposure? If so, you bomb on this test.**

ReMedy: **Wear white panties with white clothes. If your pants are so tight that you can see the outline of your panties, try buying one size larger.**

Test: Spring Valley

Target question: "Is my shirt too tight?"

Action: The girls are probably not quite ready for this test, so we'll let the moms take it. You might start by acknowledging that "we are girls and women, and we'll all be getting or already have breasts!" (The girls will giggle something silly!) Have the moms place the tips of their fingers together and press into their shirts right in the "valley" between the breasts. Count to three and have them take their fingers away. If their shirts spring back like a mini-trampoline, they're too tight. Explain to the girls that even though this might not be a problem for them just yet, it won't be long until they need to be careful about wearing shirts that are too tight.

Remedy: Don't buy clothes based on size. Buy them based on fit. Usually, you have to go a few sizes larger these days to have a modest fit.

Test: Over & Out

Target question: "Is my shirt too low?"

Action: Lean forward a little bit. Can you see too much chest skin or future cleavage? If so, your shirt is too low.

Remedy: Today's fashions thrive on low shirts. Layering them is often the only remedy. Throw a little T-shirt under a rugby, and you have a great look.

Is My Swimsuit Modest?

Oh, girlfriend! That is a hard question. I would say that your swimsuit needs to pass nearly all of these tests. Can you raise and praise without showing off your belly? Can you bend over without showing off cleavage? Can you sit with your legs crisscrossed and look in a mirror without your suit gapping at the crotch? And still...swimsuits aren't high on the modesty scale unless you're in the water! So when you jump out, don't flaunt your body—instead, cover up with a simple pair of shorts and a T-shirt or one of the cute little cover-ups available today!

SKG Challenge
30–45 Minutes

After you have completed the Girl Gab somewhere, go over these simple challenge rules before you set the girls loose.

A. Shop as a group, allowing the girls' opinions to encourage and direct each other for what they think looks cool and is trendy.

B. Everything they buy has to pass all of the Truth or Bare Fashion Tests learned on this date and "Today's Hot Looks" tests from the previous date (see page 80). The mothers will act as a panel of judges!

Now, present them with their cash and try to keep up!

Be prepared to say "no" to any outfits that do not pass the tests. Also, be prepared to pep them up and redirect them if they get discouraged. This date is not about saying "no" to immodesty. It's about saying "yes" to cool, godly clothes and creating positive peer pressure!

SKG Radio
3 Minutes

Use your SKG audio files to tune in to another recording artist for some big sister advice!

SKG Driveway Prayer
3–5 Minutes

Before you split up, ask all the girls to pray in their driveways with their moms tonight. Pray for each girl, and ask that in the years ahead, these girls would be a positive influence on one another in every way.

Internal Fashion

 Challenge activity:
A new hairstyle or updo

Key verse: 1 Corinthians 11:8-10

Key thought: My beauty is ultimately determined by what I wear on the *inside*.

Suggested challenge setting: A hair salon

SKG Prep Talk

I'd admired her from a distance for years. I'd never spent much time around her. I'd just run into her at church, Bible school, or the grocery store. She had the most adorable dimples and perky blue eyes.

Then one day I showed up at the pool, and there she was.

"Get away," she snarled at her little son. Profanity followed as she grumbled about how he'd gotten her book wet.

I was shocked. Surely I'd just caught her on a bad day.

A few weeks later, there she was again, sunning herself by the pool and ignoring her kids. I watched when she and her friend began to gather the kids for lunch. One straggler found the water much too tempting and stayed in the pool giggling.

The mom stomped over to the edge and began to bellow expletives at her poor little son. He didn't seem shocked. It looked like Mom's ranting and cursing was just par for the course.

The aura of beauty began to disappear.

It was soon hard to even remember what it looked like.

We all know people who appear beautiful until we begin to see inside of them. Then the beauty quickly fades. Conversely, other people seem to grow more and more beautiful as we see deeper into their hearts.

Which kind of person are you?

Which one is your daughter becoming?

Prep Talk with God

Ask the Lord to help you focus more energy on adorning your daughter's heart than on filling her closet and drawers.

Planning Date #7

Internal Beauty

Subject: Showing your beauty through submission

Setting Options: A hair salon or the home of a friend who does great updos!

Materials you'll need at your destination:

- The salon or specialist should supply everything you need
- This book

This date is about teaching your daughter that God has "garments" for us to wear that give us internal beauty. We'll do this by focusing on hair, since both the Old and New Testament have encouragements for women to allow their hair to be an expression of the internal garment of submission.[11] You'll have a great time at a hair salon, where your daughter can learn more about how to care for her hair and can be treated to a new cut or an updo.

Select your destination. Find a hair salon that's cool and fun to go to. Spend some time on the phone explaining to the stylist that this is a special date for you and your daughter and explain that you'd like to...

> **A.** encourage your daughter by sharing what's beautiful about her hair
>
> **B.** train her to take care of her hair

Read over the SKG Challenge so you can be prepared or so you can prepare your salon specialist to go over areas suggested in the challenge.

Budget Cruncher

The purpose of this night is to focus on your daughter's hair. If taking her to a salon is entirely too expensive, first see if you can find someone at church who is either a stylist or just has a reputation for great French braids or other hairstyles and would be willing to invite you over for your special time of encouragement. If that doesn't work, try borrowing a book from the library that has directions for special braids or hair wraps. Learn something special you can do to surprise your daughter.

SKG Radio
7–10 Minutes

Play "Date #7: Internal Fashion" from your SKG audio file as you drive to your destination.

SKG Challenge
30–45 Minutes

Prepare yourself, your salon stylist, or whomever is leading the challenge portion to accomplish the following during your daughter's haircut/style or updo.

1. *Teach her basic hair care.* At this age, many of our daughters think a fun hairstyle is cool if they are in the mood…but most of the time when the brush comes out, they grumble! So empower her to be the one to take care of her hair. Here are the basic guidelines:

- Shampoo whenever your hair starts to look stringy or feel oily. That's usually several times a week by the time a girl is eight to twelve. For active girls and girls with oily hair, it may be daily.

- Use a pH-balanced shampoo and squirt about the size of a quarter into your hand. Work it through your hair by massaging with your fingertips, not by scratching with your fingernails.

- Rinse thoroughly until there's nothing at all left. If you have shampoo left in your hair, it'll just get dirtier faster, and you'll be doing it again very soon!

- Brush your hair at least twice daily…when you wake up and before you go to sleep. It's a good idea to give it a fresh brushing after you swim or play sports or if you're going to be doing something special like going to a friend's house for a while.

2. *Discuss a fun new haircut* or a special braid or updo—and let the stylist do her work!

SKG Girl Gab
15–25
Minutes

After your daughter has been made to look and feel lovely, it's time to find a place to be alone with her. Most likely, you'll need to drive somewhere else. Play a favorite CD of hers on the way. Or you can begin the conversation time while you drive.

This Girl Gab hits some heavy teaching on submission, but I believe our girls are ready for it. After you've completed the Submission Scale quiz, take time to talk about what you can both specifically do to demonstrate a submissive spirit.

Your daughter's "Girl Gab" for this date is on page 185.

Date #7: Internal Fashion

Girl Gab

Ever meet a girl who just looked so cool but then turned out to be a snob? Notice how her beauty fades? Of course, maybe you've also met a girl who at first glance doesn't seem that beautiful, but the more you're around her, the more fabulous she looks to you. That's internal beauty you're seeing. A Secret Keeper Girl isn't complete without fashion for her heart.

> *"Man did not come from woman, but woman from man;*
> *neither was man created for woman, but woman for*
> *man. For this reason, and because of the angels, the*
> *woman ought to have a sign of authority on her head."*
> *1 Corinthians 11:8-10*

Women in Bible days were so committed to the internal fashion of submission that they wore their hair a certain way—or had some kind of hat on—as an external reminder for themselves and everyone else around them. Wow! Don't you think it'd be cool if our culture cared so much about how we looked on the inside that we wore a symbol of it on the outside? We don't do that anymore, and I don't think it's necessary, but I do like the idea that both men and women understood the idea of mutual respect and submission.

Fashion for My Heart

Clothes aren't the only things we wear. God invites us to "wear" things on the inside too. Check out these verses and discover some of the hottest fashions for the heart. Underline the things we're called to "wear."

"[A woman of God] is clothed
with strength and dignity."
Proverbs 31:25

"Put on the full armor of God...Stand firm then, with
the belt of truth buckled around your waist, with the
breastplate of righteousness in place, and with your
feet fitted with the readiness that comes from the
gospel of peace. In addition to all this, take the shield
of faith, with which you can extinguish all the flaming
arrows of the evil one. Take the helmet of salvation and
the sword of the Spirit, which is the word of God."
Ephesians 6:13-17

"I…want women to dress modestly, with decency…with good deeds appropriate for women who profess to worship God."
1 Timothy 2:9-10

"Your beauty should not come from outward adornment…[but from] a gentle and quiet spirit."
1 Peter 3:3-4

The things you've underlined are all vital parts of a Secret Keeper Girl's wardrobe. The most vital internal garment for you is submission. Submission is allowing someone else to lead you. Submitting doesn't require you to mindlessly follow a bad example. Submission invites you to sometimes let a good friend get to play the game she wants to play even if you'd rather not. Submission requires you to quietly honor your parents, teachers, and other authorities with obedience. What a privilege! (What a tough task!) So how do you know if you're wearing it? It's not like you can see it. Let's see if you've got submission hanging in your internal power wardrobe.

Submission Scale Quiz

Circle the statement that sounds most like you.

1. When the kids I'm hanging with decide they want to do something I don't want to do, I
   a. yell and grumble and run home stomping all the way
   b. keep talking until I convince everyone to do what I want to do
   c. try to listen to everyone's feelings and help all of us work it out—even though this is hard to do
   d. do what my friends prefer—after all, everyone deserves a turn to lead

2. When the teacher gives me homework, I usually
   a. refuse to do it
   b. do it, but the whole time I think it's dumb because I already know it all
   c. wish I didn't have to, but I don't want to disappoint my teacher
   d. do it without thinking too much—after all, she's the teacher!

3. When my parents ask me to do something, I
   a. throw a royal fit and ask to be paid
   b. grumble and do it half right
   c. feel sad because I'm not getting to do what I want, but I get it done
   d. do it with all my heart because I want to please my parents

4. When my brother or sister wants the same video game or toy that I want, I

    a. tease him or her the whole time as I play with the toy

    b. tell him what I think he should be doing

    c. ask if I can have it first, and let the other person wait for his or her turn

    d. let the other person go first and find something else to do

5. When I think someone has made a mistake, I

    a. want to be the first to correct the person, and I do it as loudly as possible

    b. try to take over because I can do it better

    c. watch for a good time to bring it up quietly

    d. wait for adults or others in authority to make things right

6. I go to church because

    a. my parents make me, but I wouldn't if I could help it

    b. I have to, but I never really learn anything

    c. I have good friends there

    d. I want to be what God wants me to be, and church is a great place to learn this

So, how'd ya do? Count up all your a's, b's, c's, and d's.
Write the totals below.

_____A_____B_____C_____D

Which letter did you have the most of? Circle that letter below to find out how you're doing.

D. Submissive Servant

Wow! I wish I could score this high. Keep up the great work. Just don't let it go to your head.

C. Sensitive Socialite

Good eye, girlfriend. You recognize your own desires, but you're trying hard to put others ahead of yourself, and you often succeed.

B. Boisterous Boss

Try harder! You probably have a lot of leadership potential, but God can't use that until you learn some gentleness. Work on controlling your tongue.

A. Raging Rebel

Uh-oh! Watch out! You're wearing the wrong stuff, girl. You need to work on controlling your tongue and your emotions.

SKG Radio
3 Minutes

Turn up the volume on your SKG audio files to hear a great Christian recording artist weigh in!

As you arrive home, ask the Lord to give you both a submissive spirit, especially in the home. If you need to, confess to the Lord that this has been an area of sin in your life. Give your daughter that same chance.

SKG Driveway Prayer
3–5 Minutes

Affirmation of Beauty

Challenge activity:
A dress-up date with Dad (and Mom!) to affirm your beauty

Key verse: **Psalm 139:13-16**

Key thought: **God calls me a princess.**

Suggested challenge setting: **An upscale restaurant**

Special needs: **Dad (or a grandpa or a big brother)**

SKG Prep Talk

It was Lexi's fifth birthday.

My mother and I were sitting at the kitchen table sipping tea and giggling about the day's events when Bob, my husband, walked in. I glanced at my watch. He was awfully late.

He looked like the cat that had caught the mouse...only this mouse must've been quite a prize. He beamed as he walked over to Lexi and presented her with something.

He had all of our attention now.

Her awkward fingers lifted the lid from a tiny heart-shaped pewter box and grasped the shiny gold bracelet laden with blue gems.

"Read the box," Bob encouraged her, looking at me. I reached for the box and read the inscription: *For Lexi from Daddy, December 28, 1998: "Something Blue."*

Tears fell down my cheeks as I shared it with my mother. Our hearts knew the significance of this precious gift, even if Lexi's bright blue eyes were simply curious and excited.

Bob has given Lexi a special gift every five years on her birthday. So far, she's received three gifts that represent each phrase of the old bride's poem: "Something old, something new, something borrowed, something blue"!

We laugh and say that it's our way of bribing her, because she won't be ready for marriage until she's at least 20. But it's a special love connection between Lexi and her daddy. It's an affirmation of her value and his dreams for her.

Prep Talk with God

Ask the Lord to move in the relationship between your daughter and her father. Ask Him to overcome every obstacle and create a special newness in their relationship through this date. Spend an extra amount of time praying if your daughter's father is not involved for some reason. If you've decided to ask a grandfather or big brother or uncle or close friend to participate, pray over them and ask God to begin to use them to bless your daughter like a dad can. (And you can be absolutely certain that God is a father to the fatherless. He's got your back, my friend.)

Planning Date #8:

Affirmation of Beauty

Subject: A dress-up date with Dad to affirm your daughter's beauty

Setting: A posh restaurant

Special needs: Dad (or a grandpa or big brother or close friend)

Materials you'll need at your destination:

- Reservations at an upscale restaurant
- A small, special box
- This book
- A special gift for your daughter (optional)

I want to bring your daughter's dad into the picture to help affirm her beauty. Social surveys demonstrate that girls who have no connectedness with their fathers tend to be more likely to act out high-risk behaviors as teens. On the other hand, girls who have a close relationship with their dads are more likely to live a life of purity, avoid substance abuse, and be generally well-adjusted as teens. (I always encourage dads of teen girls to make sure their daughters get at least one big hug a day!) The purpose of this date is to let you and your husband evaluate this important factor in your daughter's life and to give you a good opportunity to just let dad love her with his time, energy, and focus.

To prepare for this date, first make reservations at someplace very upscale, and see to babysitting or alternate plans for any siblings. This night is for just you, her, and Dad.

After you've got your reservation, there's only one thing to prepare: The Box of Questions. You'll be playing a game at the restaurant using these. First, turn to pages 191–192 and cut the questions into tiny strips. Then find or make a really special box to place them in. You might find a little jewelry box and wrap it in festive paper, or you can purchase a little ceramic box that can be a gift to your daughter at the end of the game. It just needs to be fun and special. *(Note: Please read through all of the questions to make sure you're comfortable with them. If for some reason your daughter's father will be replaced by a grandfather, a big brother, an uncle, or a close friend, please write your own questions using these as guides.)*

I want you and your daughter to go all out in dressing up for this date. Why? Well, it seems that even girls who generally dress

modestly throw all caution to the wind when they prepare for special occasions. Spaghetti straps, skirts slit up to the thigh, backless gowns, and teeny-tiny mini-dresses fail every SKG Truth or Bare Fashion Test. Take this opportunity to remind your daughter that modesty applies in all settings.

Your SKG Challenge is the dinner date. At a more elegant restaurant this will take longer than 45 minutes, so your Girl Gab is rolled into the Challenge in the form of the Box of Questions. In her scrapbook, if your daughter is keeping one, she can find a place to record the special things you or her dad said during this time in the restaurant.

Okay, check your lipstick and let's go!

SKG Radio
7–10
Minutes

Play "Date #8: Affirmation of Beauty" from your SKG audio file as you drive to your destination.

SKG
Challenge
1 Hour and
20 Minutes +

Get seated and order dinner before you present the SKG Girl Gab Box of Questions. Explain that this is a game you'll be playing. Here's how it works:

1. Take turns pulling questions from the box. The person who pulls it tells who it's for—Dad, Mom, or daughter—and reads it.

2. The person it's directed to needs to do what is asked of him or her. Most are recalling memories or sharing opinions, so you can't get them right or wrong. But a few questions are to test how well you know each other. If you get one of these wrong, you have to put it back to try again if it comes up.

3. The person with the most slips before your entrees arrive gets to select a dessert to share.

SKG Girl Gab

Your Girl Gab for this date is the Box of Questions. After the date, you might give them to your daughter to put in her scrapbook if she is making one.

Pop in your SKG audio file for the ride home. A Christian recording artist will share her beauty secrets.

SKG Radio
3 Minutes

SKG Driveway Prayer
5–7 Minutes

Ask your husband to pray over your daughter to complete your date and your SKG experience. His prayer should affirm both her internal and external beauty.

Your daughter's "Girl Gab" for this date is on page 191.

Box of Questions for Date #8:

Girl Gab

Affirmation of Beauty

Dad: "God carefully and precisely created your daughter to be beautiful. Describe the first moment you saw her."

Dad: "Your daughter has been learning that internal beauty is more important than external beauty. What's the most beautiful thing about her heart?"

Dad: "Your daughter has been learning that her body has the power to intoxicate guys. Tell her your perspective as a dad on how a guy thinks about girls."

Dad: "Beauty is the unique features about us that no one else has. What unique feature or features about your wife attracted you to her?"

Mom: "How did you tell your daughter's dad that you were pregnant with her?"

Mom: "What part of your daughter's face most looks like you? What part most looks like her dad?"

Mom: "What's your daughter's favorite book?"

Daughter: "What's the most fun you've ever had with your dad? Why?"

Daughter: "When do you most sense your dad's love? Is it a) when he hugs you or b) when he does things with you? Why?"

Daughter: "Fill in the blank. 'My beauty is ultimately determined by

_____.'"

Daughter: "Tell your dad about the effect of the Gestalt theory. (Possible answer: "The human brain craves the completion of an incomplete image, so although sometimes we can see only a couple of curvy lines and a dot, our minds create the image of a person.") How does this relate to fashion?"

Daughter: "Tell your mom and dad which SKG date was your favorite and why."

Daughter: "Name three internal fashions we should wear." (Possible answers: submission, good deeds, a gentle spirit, truth, strength, dignity, and so on.)

Part 3

Devotions and Other Good Stuff

Secret Keeper Girl Devotions

Secret Keeper Girl FAQs

Notes

Girl Gab Pullouts

Secret Keeper GIRL
Devotions

Week 1

Okay, moms and daughters. Here ya go! This is all the devo power you need to have some great mother–daughter times together for the next 20 days or so, depending on how many days you take off. (You are allowed two a week if you want them!) Just keep this book handy, and dive into your time together by reading aloud together!

Week One / Day One
In the Morning I Lay My Requests Before You

"In the morning, O LORD, you hear my voice; in the morning I lay my requests before you and wait in expectation."

PSALM 5:3

I don't know about you, but I'm not much of a morning person. In fact, I can be downright grumpy. But a number of years ago God showed me the verse above and others like it. "In the morning, O LORD, you hear my voice; in the morning, I lay my requests before you and wait in expectation." Was God really calling *me* to get out of bed a few minutes earlier to talk to Him? I confessed to Him that I wasn't sure I could do it and I needed His gentle, loving help.

The most amazing thing happened the very next morning. My alarm went off to get me up to do my devotions and I really, really wanted to go back to sleep. But suddenly I heard a tapping at my back door. *Who could be at my back door so early?* I thought. I dragged myself out of bed, only to find no one there. I crawled back into my warm, comfy bed, only to have that tapping rudely call me to check the back door again. I got there, and *no one* was there. I went back into my room and waited, thinking someone must be playing a trick on me.

Soon, the tapping started again. I got down on all fours and sneaked out under my dining-room table. I was staring at my glass door, when I saw the most amazing thing. A tiny bird was sitting on my deck tapping on the glass. *Ha! What a funny way for God to awaken me,* I thought. *How tender! How loving! How hilarious!* That little bird came back every morning for the next three days, luring me out of bed. (One morning I even had Robby and Lexi sneak out with me to see him so people would actually believe me!) I believe that was God's big answer to me—He really does want my attention first thing in the morning. I confess it has been hard for me, but since that little bird visited my deck I've been giving my best effort to hear God's voice *in the morning!*

In your journal today:

Copy Psalm 5:3 into your journal and write a prayer to God asking Him to help you to talk to Him "in the morning."

Week One / Day Two
Earnestly I Seek You
Read Psalm 63

*"O God, You are my God, earnestly I seek
You; my soul thirsts for You."*
PSALM 63:1

I have a missionary friend named John, who went to a Spanish-speaking country to help build a church. Most of the crew were not Christians, but John wanted to share God's love with them, so he built the church with them. They taught him some Spanish so they could communicate better. One day the missionary supervisor came to see how John was doing. He heard John ask for the hammer, and the other guys giggled. He heard him ask for a saw and, again, the guys giggled. The missionary looked concerned. He pulled John to the side and asked him why he was calling the workers bad names when he asked for things. My friend looked over at the workers, who were howling with laughter. The joke was on him. He didn't know Spanish, and so he didn't know he was actually saying, "Pass the hammer, jerk!" or "Pass the saw, loser!"

Sometimes we have a translation difficulty with the Bible. You see, it wasn't actually written in English. It was written in Hebrew, Greek, and Aramaic. Translating the Bible into English from these very complicated languages was a big task, and so sometimes we get a very simplified version or a version that just doesn't say what God actually meant for us to know. That's why you must study diligently. Today's memory verse is a good example of what I'm talking about. Read the verse at the top of the page.

The word "earnestly" is actually the Hebrew word *shachar,* which means "dawn, early, rising in immediate pursuit." In other words, talking to God should be the very first thing we do in the day. If your morning routine is so rushed that you can't spend time with God, try to get up a little earlier. If you're just "not a morning person" it's okay to have your quiet time with God later in the day, but be sure to utter a prayer to give Him your day as you awaken!

In your journal today:

Copy Psalm 63:1 into your journal. Write about a day when you really felt "thirsty" for God. What did that feel like? Tell Him!

Week One / Day Three
Seek First the Kingdom of God
Read Matthew 6:25-34

"Seek first his kingdom and his righteousness, and all these things will be given to you as well."
MATTHEW 6:33

When I was not much older than you, I felt like God wanted me to help a ministry teach children about Jesus. I wasn't old enough to actually be a teacher, so I volunteered to be a helper. That same summer a lot of my friends were going to the beach every day and planning a lot of cool things. I felt a little left out, but I kept believing that when I sought God's kingdom first, "all these things" would be given to me as well. For me at that age, "all these things" meant some fun and sun. That summer God blessed me amazingly with a scholarship to the most awesome Christian camp near Pittsburgh. I got to go caving, rock climbing, and horseback riding. I tried my hand at archery, self-defense, candlemaking, and all kinds of stuff. It was so amazing. God really does bless our socks off when we seek His kingdom first.

How do you think God wants you to seek His kingdom? Is there a friend who isn't the most fun to be with but needs your love right now? Is there someone you need to pray for more?

What are "all these things" in your heart? They're different for all of us. Is it a happier home? Is it a better teacher? Is it more friends? Is it a certain thing you're hoping to do?

Guess what? God already knows about it, and so you might as well tell Him.

In your journal today:

Copy Matthew 6:33 into your journal. Write a prayer asking God to show you how you can seek His kingdom, and ask Him to help you to do that first rather than trying to get "all these things"! Trust Him to provide them or to change your heart.

Week One / Day Four
Behold, I Stand at the Door and Knock
Read Revelation 3:14-22

"Here I am! I stand at the door and knock. If anyone hears My voice and opens the door, I will come in and eat with him, and he with Me."

REVELATION 3:20

There is a story about a family who was trapped by a flood. They prayed for God to rescue them. Soon a boat floated by and a man offered to pick them up. The family said, "No, it's okay—we're waiting for God to rescue us!" After a while longer, a helicopter came by and dropped down a lifeline. The family refused it because they were waiting for God. Hello! Do you think that just maybe God had sent that boat and that helicopter?

Today's verse talks about God standing at the door and knocking. A lot of people use this verse to explain that Jesus is talking to unbelievers and saying He wants to be with them. It's true that He wants to be in every person's life. But look at the heading just before verse 14. In my Bible it says, "To the *church* in Laodicea"! This verse is written to those who already believe that Jesus is their Savior. And it says, "Here I am! I stand at the door and knock... open the door!" Sometimes as believers we really need to slow down and realize that God needs us to respond to something He's already doing in our lives.

Is there something you've been praying about for a while? Is it possible that God has already sent a boat or a helicopter to say, "Here I am"? Take a moment today to look around to see where God is knocking at the door of your life.

In your journal today:

Copy Revelation 3:20 into your journal. Sit quietly before God today and just let Him reveal to you where maybe He's been knocking at the door of your life. After you do this, write about what God tells you.

Week One / Day Five
Look at Us!
Read Acts 3:1-10

"Peter looked straight at him, as did John.
Then Peter said, 'Look at us!'"
ACTS 3:4

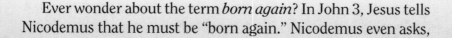

Ever wonder about the term *born again*? In John 3, Jesus tells Nicodemus that he must be "born again." Nicodemus even asks,

"How can an old man get back into his mother's belly?" (See verse 4.) But Jesus is talking about something spiritual, something we can't see, not crawling back into our moms' bellies to get reborn. What does it mean?

Well, pretend with me for a moment that you are a baby still cradled in your mother's warm, wet belly. You are fully developed and ready to be born. You can even hear the distant world outside your mother's belly. But what of that world can you see? Nothing, right? No brilliant colors. No sunshine. No rainbows. No smiling faces. No acts of love. You cannot see until you are born. Then suddenly the wonders of this world are fully exposed for you to see.

It's like that for people who don't know Jesus as their Lord and Savior. They just don't "get it" sometimes because they cannot "see" what you see in the spirit world. They can't see God's love. Can't see God's healing. Can't see the warmth of fellowship in a Bible-study group. They haven't been born into that world yet.

What *can* they see? They can see you! Our Bible reading today tells about a man who needed physical healing. It's funny that Peter says, "Look at us!" Why didn't he say, "Look at God"? Two reasons. One, the man wasn't a believer yet, and so he was blind to God. But also, because Peter and John were living so very much as God wanted them to, they could confidently say, "Look at us!" knowing that the man would see proof of God. Is your life like that? Can your friends who can't see God see proof of Him in your life?

In your journal today:

Copy Acts 3:4 into your journal. In your journal, write a prayer of confession admitting what areas of your life need to better reflect God. Then, ask God to help you to be more like Him in that area so others can see God's power in your life.

Week 2

Week Two / Day One
Seeing God in His Creation

"I lift up my eyes to the hills—
where does my help come from?
My help comes from the Lord, the
Maker of heaven and earth."
PSALM 121:1-2

A number of years ago, I was sitting on the beach feeling very sad. I was sitting right where the foam and waves just touch the sand, making it smooth like cement when they subside back into the ocean. I was wondering if God even cared about me because I was so discouraged. So I asked Him. "God, do You even care?"

Suddenly my eye caught some movement on that smooth sand. I moved closer. This time when the waves came up I saw clearly that dozens upon dozens of teeny-tiny clams were being washed onshore. A few seconds after the water subsided, they all suddenly stood on end like tiny little soldiers and wriggled their way down into the depths of the cool sand. I thought this was amazing that God had created these teeny-tiny, insignificant creatures with a way to protect themselves from drying out in the hot sun. Suddenly, it hit me. If God cares about those little clams, of course He cares about me! It was like a big hug from God.

The Bible is full of God communicating to people He loves through His creation.

This week, we're going to look at some ways that God speaks to us through creation...and to Y-O-U! You might want to plan to have your devotions outside or near a window so you can be close to creation when you are talking to God.

In your journal today:

Copy Psalm 121:1-2 into your journal and write a prayer to God asking Him to help you notice Him in creation this week. Maybe write about a time when you remember seeing Him in what He has made.

Week Two / Day Two
Burning Off the Chaff
Read Luke 3:15-18

"He will burn up the chaff with unquenchable fire."
LUKE 3:17

In Australia there are great, horrible "bush" fires. (We might compare them to forest fires.) When I was visiting there, I sat in a restaurant overlooking a valley that had been entirely burned out. The flames had obviously come within feet of the restaurant. I asked my tour guide, "How do they fight the fire?" He replied, "We don't. It's too powerful, and its purpose is really to make the bush stronger—so it must burn." He went on to explain that the trees making up the bush had a cone so hard and so thick that the only thing that would allow the seed to pop out and begin to grow was intense heat. When the cones heated up, they burst, and the bush could continue growing. The fire also burned off the weak, dry, and dying trees. So you see, the fire is actually a good thing.

John the Baptist said something about fire when the people asked him if he was "the Christ." He said that Jesus would burn up the chaff (the useless, inedible stuff that's left after wheat is harvested—yuck!) with unquenchable fire. In other words, in your life and mine Jesus might sometimes let things get really hard and difficult for us. He does this to burn off the useless things in our lives (the chaff) and to let seeds of growth sprout in us.

Has your family ever been through a hard time? Have you ever wondered why God was allowing it? Wait until you see what God allows to grow in your life before you question what God was up to. It's usually something really good.

In your journal today:

Copy Luke 3:17. Write a prayer to God asking Him to help you to endure the "fire" of something that is really hard for you right now.

Tell God that you'll trust Him to make something good grow as He burns away the useless things in your life.

Week Two / Day Three
Even a Donkey
Read Numbers 22:21-35

"The donkey saw me and turned away from me these three times. If she had not turned away, I would certainly have killed you by now, but I would have spared her."
NUMBERS 22:33

When was the last time you saw a donkey speak? (Maybe when you watched one of the *Shrek* movies, but hey...they're only cartoons!) In the Bible, God actually caused a donkey to talk. He used this little creature to both rescue and direct the man named Balaam. Balaam was going somewhere God didn't want him to go. God was allowing him to go as long as he said only what God wanted him to say.

But Balaam struck out on his journey as if he was "the man."

God sent an angel to get his attention, but only Balaam's donkey saw him. How many times? Three times! And then, the donkey talked! (Would you have thought you were losing your mind or what?)

My friend, God used a mere donkey. Is He not going to mightily use you also during the course of your life? Oh, He certainly is. Ephesians 4:7 says, "He has given each of us a special gift according to the generosity of Christ" (NLT). Jesus has given you a special gift…or ability…that no one else quite has. (Kind of like giving the gift of speech to a donkey!) He's going to use you in a mighty, magnificent, and powerful way if you will let Him. After all, you are one of His most magnificent creations!

In your journal today:

Copy Ephesians 4:7 into your journal. Write a prayer asking God to use you and to help you to see the special gift or ability He has given to you. (It could take a long time to see it. I found my gift when I was 26, but I had a hint about it when I was 8!)

Week Two / Day Four

Note: It's best if you do this devotion outside during daylight when you can do some bird-watching!

Soar on Wings Like Eagles
Read Isaiah 40:26-31

"Those who hope in the LORD will renew their strength. They will soar on wings like eagles; they will run and not grow weary, they will walk and not be faint."
ISAIAH 40:31

Today is a good day to have your devotions outside if you can. If you can't, move to a window. I'm praying even now as I write this that the Lord will show you the most beautiful bird today. I'm praying that you'll be able to see one in flight. If you can, go outside and watch and wait for one to fly above you.

Just sit quietly and think about God as you watch birds nearby. Imagine that this is the freedom with which He wants you to live every day. Let Him speak to you.

Week Two / Day Five
The Circle of the Earth
Read Isaiah 40:21-22

"He sits enthroned above the circle of the earth."
Isaiah 40:22

How do you know that this Bible you're reading is real and true and is written by God? Think about it for a minute. It's a hard question to answer, isn't it? Oh my sweet friend, all of your life you will be searching for more and more proof that this Bible is real. And today I want to show you a secret treasure in the Bible that helps us to know that it is.

Read Isaiah 40:22 again. Where does it say that God sits? Above the circle of the earth, right? Wait a minute! This book was written when many people believed the earth was *flat!* How on earth did the writer know that the earth was a circle? (It would be many years before anyone guessed that the earth was round, and when they did, people tried to kill them because it was so unbelievable to them!) This Bible verse can only be explained by one thing. The God of the universe who created the earth and knew it was a circle must have inspired the writer to say such a thing.

Astronaut John Glenn was a Christian. He said that he knew the moment he believed that Jesus was the Christ. It was when he was in outer space looking through a tiny window in his spacecraft back to the round, quiet earth. He thought of this Bible verse and suddenly realized, "God had to have inspired that truth!"

You can be certain that God *is*—and that what He has inspired in the Bible is absolutely true.

In your journal today:

Copy Isaiah 40:22 into your journal. In your journal, write a prayer of praise to God that is three sentences long. Use only things about creation to praise Him. Be creative!

Week 3

Week Three / Day One
Praise God with Your Tongue!

"Whoever would love life and see good days must keep his tongue from evil and his lips from deceitful speech."
1 PETER 3:10

Okay—you may have already figured this out, but you're a girl! (What a concept!) As a girl you tend to talk a whole lot more than you would if you were a guy. Seriously, people have studied this. In one study, they watched preschoolers play. The boys? They were making all kinds of gross and loud noises. You can only imagine! The girls? Well, they were conversing as if they could fix all the problems in the world! In a study of adults they found that the average man speaks something like 10,000 words a day. Now that's a lot, but a woman speaks almost three times that many words. Talking is good, but God's Word tells us again and again that talking is something we have to be very careful with. So we're going to spend all week talking to God about talking.

For today, I want you to praise God for the gift of speech. (Isn't it interesting that we praise God with talking?) Go ahead! I want you to write a nice loooooong letter of praise to God. Just so you have an example, here's my praise to God for creating speech.

"O God, I thank You that You've given me the ability to speak. I praise You that I can tell my kids I love them. I praise You that I can sing songs of worship. I'm thankful I can giggle and tell jokes. God, let my lips always be a blessing to You!"

In your journal today:

Copy 1 Peter 3:10 into your journal and write your praise to God for your ability to speak.

Week Three / Day Two
Taming the Tongue
Read James 3:3-6

"When we put bits into the mouths of horses to make them obey us, we can turn the whole animal."
JAMES 3:3

Once I was riding horseback with my friend in Missouri. It was all going along very nicely until I turned my horse around to head home. That crazy animal couldn't wait to get there, I guess. It took off at lightning speed, and I was scared silly. I thought surely I would fall off, and so I tried to slow that beast down with the bridle and reins. But nothing worked. Eventually I just held on and enjoyed the ride! I just couldn't control the animal.

The Bible tells us that sometimes our tongues are like that.

Uncontrollable. Girls sometimes struggle with this. I heard about two girls who showed up at youth group one night with almost exactly the same new haircut. One girl squinted her eyes and said, "She's always trying to copy me. She did this on purpose." How silly. (And stupid.) But it was just enough to make the second girl feel really bad and use a few cruel words of her own.

Have you ever had a friend say cruel things to you? Do you remember how it made you feel? It hurts, doesn't it?

God wants you to control your mouth just like a bit controls a horse. Do you need to work on this area of your life?

In your journal today:

Copy James 3:3 and then confess to God a time that your tongue was out of control and you said something unkind to someone.

Ask God to forgive you and to help you be kind.

Week Three / Day Three
Lying and Dying
Read Psalm 119:33-40

"Truth lasts; lies are here today and gone tomorrow."
PROVERBS 12:19 MSG

One time I was asking God to show me if there were any lies in my life. I felt God telling me that I needed to be free of lying, but I just couldn't think why He was talking to me about it. I prayed that He would show me.

The next day my mom brought out a beautiful clay pot I had made in seventh grade. Only...I hadn't made it. I always felt so good when I'd bring home a really neat art project and she would praise it, so one day I brought home a piece of art I didn't make.

Not only had I stolen it, but I'd lived with the lie of it for years. Soon I was confessing it to my mom and being set free from a lie told long ago.

You know, God doesn't like lying. That's why old Ananias and Sapphira fell down dead…because they lied. Sometimes a lie can be big and bad like the one I told about the pot. Or sometimes it can be an exaggeration, such as "I was on my best behavior in lunch today" when you really were a part of the group that got in trouble. Or a lie can be failing to speak up in truth, like when a teacher asks who did something bad in class and you just don't say anything even though you know. God doesn't mess with lying. He hates it.

But He loves truth. Is there an area in your life where you need to work on being more truthful?

In your journal today:

Copy Proverbs 12:19 and then write to God about a time that you were not truthful. If it involves your parents, please go to them and confess it to them also.

Week Three / Day Four
To Give Courage

"By all this we are encouraged. In addition to our own encouragement, we were especially delighted to see how happy Titus was, because his spirit has been refreshed by all of you. I had boasted to him about you, and you have not embarrassed me. But just as everything we said to you was true, so our boasting about you to Titus has proved to be true as well."

2 CORINTHIANS 7:13-14

Today's devotion is just a touch…a peek…into the apostle Paul's pride over his friends in Corinth. See how he uses words like "encourage" and "boasted" and "delighted"!

One day when I was a little down, Lexi sneaked off, bought a special card, and wrote me a note of encouragement. It changed my whole week!

God wants you to be an encourager. (*To encourage* means "to give courage.") For devotions today, I want you to write a nice note to a friend encouraging her for being a good Christian. Or if the friend you're writing to isn't a Christian, thank her for being a good friend. Be specific about what you're thanking her for—what do you like about her?

In your journal today:

No journal writing. Write a note and give it to a friend.

Week Three / Day Five
Confession

*"Confess your sins to each other and pray for
each other so that you may be healed."*
JAMES 5:16

Sin makes us sick. Some kinds of sin make us physically sick, but all kinds of sin make us emotionally sick. Can you remember ever feeling really bad about something you had done wrong? Well, today I want to share with you God's prescription for that sickness. James 5:16 tells us that when we confess our sins to each other, we are healed. Now don't be confused. Only God can forgive your sins, and don't let anyone tell you otherwise. But He has given us each other here on earth to help with the hurt. So the healing for the sickness that sin causes comes from telling someone. (And that someone can help you not to do the same thing again.)

Secrets aren't a good thing when it comes to sin. I remember keeping a secret from my mom for years about a bad thing I did. I was so ashamed. I felt lonely and sad about it. Then one day I managed to tell her about it, and suddenly I felt great. My mom wasn't super mad like I thought she'd be. She was a little disappointed, but she helped me figure out why I had sinned like this and make decisions so I wouldn't do it again. Don't let another day go by without telling your mom about anything you've done that needs to be confessed. You'll be glad you did.

In your journal today:

Copy James 5:16. Today, write in your journal about something you need your mom's help with. Is it talking more kindly to your friends? Is it being more truthful? Confess this to her after you write about it, and watch to see how God will make your heart feel much better!

Week 4

Week Four / Day One
Looking at the Heart
Read 1 Samuel 16:2-13

"Man looks at the outward appearance,
but the LORD looks at the heart."
1 SAMUEL 16:7B

A homeless man in a small town was accused of stealing a large basket of goods from a little grocery store. The police showed up at the store with the man and the stolen things. The grocer showed much compassion. Rather than pressing charges for theft, he simply said, "Oh, I'm glad they brought you back! You left so quickly that you forgot your change." And he pulled out $38.12, gave it to the homeless man, and sent him on his way with the basket of goods.

A few days later the grocer was called in to a lawyer's office. The lawyer explained that the homeless man had died and had willed all his earthly goods to the grocer. Then he handed the grocer a dingy, dirty bag. In that bag was some old bread, a Bible, and a bank book. The last deposit in the book was for $38.12…which brought the balance to just over $3 million.

The grocer's kindness was rewarded greatly, don't you think? He didn't look at the homeless man's outward appearance—he looked at his heart and his needs. And he showed much kindness.

In our Bible reading today, you see that God did the same thing when He selected David to be king of Israel. When Samuel went to find the future king, he was at first sure God must be talking about Jesse's oldest, strongest, wisest son. But He wasn't. He was sending Samuel to select David, who was Jesse's youngest, smallest son, and who still had much to learn.

Be kind to people. You may only see how they look today, but God sees their future, and you might be an important part of it.

In your journal today:

Copy 1 Samuel 16:7b. Write a letter to God about a person in your life who needs kindness, but whose appearance is difficult for you to get past.

Week Four / Day Two
A Wall of Faith
Read Ephesians 6:10-17

*"Take up the shield of faith, with which you can extinguish
all the flaming arrows of the evil one."*
EPHESIANS 6:16

In the days of the New Testament, the armies of Rome fought a lot of terrible wars and battles. Each soldier had a shield to deflect the enemy's attack. The shield was thick and powerful, and was crafted with ridges on its sides. When the attack was particularly difficult, the Roman soldiers would lock their shields together using the ridges and grooves, linking them like puzzle pieces. They would then have an entire wall built in front of them to keep the enemy away.

Ephesians tells us that we need to have a shield of faith to protect ourselves from our enemy, Satan. It seems to me that, since the soldiers linked themselves together with their shields, God used this analogy not only to tell us to be prepared to deflect the enemy's attack, but to tell us to be prepared with friends and family members whose faith we can link into when the battle is heavy.

Which friends, family members, teachers, and church leaders do you spend time with? Are they believers whose faith is strong? If you were having a hard time, could you lock your shield of faith together with theirs?

In your journal today:

Copy Ephesians 6:16 into your journal. Write the names of the people who came to mind as you read today's devotion...people around you whose faith is strong. Thank God for them.

Week Four / Day Three
Too Much TV?
Read Psalm 119:33-37

*"Turn my eyes away from worthless things;
preserve my life according to your word."*
PSALM 119:37

My dad was the first kid on his block to have a television. (Think about it! I bet some of your grandparents never saw TV until they were your age! Strange, huh?) When I was your age, my dad had already logged a good 20 years on the tube, but one day he pulled quite a trick on me. He sat in his TV-viewing chair and said, "Watch this! Today I learned how to magically change the TV channel." Then he waved his fingers in the air and the channel would change.

I was amazed. He did this again and again—turning the TV on and off and changing channels with a flick of his fingers. The joke was on me. I was the first kid on the block to have a remote control! My dad had it hidden behind his back as he used his other hand, with "magical" fingers, to change the channels. Before that—you won't believe this—we had to actually get up off the sofa and push buttons on the television to change the channels!

Today, the average kid your age watches three hours of television a day. (That's a lot of TV!) If they keep up at that rate, they'll see nearly 8000 murders while growing up. Do you think that will affect them?

There are a lot of things in our world that can be considered "worthless things," and many of today's TV shows are among them. It can be hard to change your viewing habits if you're watching too much or watching the wrong kinds of things. You might try not watching any TV for a week. Or set a goal of only 30 minutes a day.

How are you doing? Are you filling your mind with worthless things, or are you allowing God to preserve your life with His Word?

In your journal today:

Copy Psalm 119:37 and ask God to help you to monitor your television viewing habits.

Week Four / Day Four
Keep Your Candle Burning
Read Psalm 18:28-36

*"You light my candle: the Lord my God
will enlighten my darkness."*
PSALM 18:28 NKJV

I write every book beside a candle. Somehow, candles inspire me. I just love the soft scent and the relaxing atmosphere a simple candle creates. Even if am trying to meet a deadline, a candle stills my spirit.

So I was thinking. A candle needs oxygen to burn. (It also requires fuel, such as a wick and wax, and heat.) But oxygen is the silent element. No one sees it or hears it—or goes out and finds oxygen to light a candle. You find the fuel—the candle itself—and the heat—a match. But you still must have the oxygen.

Maybe you've been to a church where you've seen someone putting candles out. They use a tool called a "candle snuffer." When it's placed over the candle, it suffocates the light by stopping oxygen from getting to the flame. The candle goes out.

In our key verse today, we see that the Lord "lights my candle." What that means is that He brings light to our life so we can see things as they are: within His loving care and provision. (We don't have to be stressed out about the mean girl at school when God gives us light to see her broken heart.) But there are things that can "snuff out" our light. For me, that can be ignoring my prayer time or spending too much time with friends who don't love God. What kind of things "snuff out" the light of God in your life?

In your journal today:

Draw a picture of a candle, then write a list of all the things in your life that could be candle snuffers. Talk to your mom about how to avoid those things.

Week Four / Day Five
You Are Beautiful
Read 1 Peter 3:3-4

"Your beauty...should be that of your inner self,
the unfading beauty of a gentle and quiet spirit,
which is of great worth in God's sight."
1 PETER 3:3-4

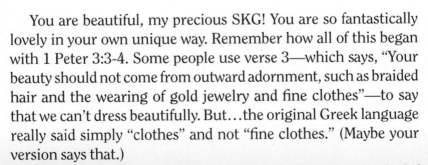

You are beautiful, my precious SKG! You are so fantastically lovely in your own unique way. Remember how all of this began with 1 Peter 3:3-4. Some people use verse 3—which says, "Your beauty should not come from outward adornment, such as braided hair and the wearing of gold jewelry and fine clothes"—to say that we can't dress beautifully. But...the original Greek language really said simply "clothes" and not "fine clothes." (Maybe your version says that.)

Anyway, the point is that we'd all be running around naked if we took this to mean God did not want us to braid our hair or wear nice clothes and jewelry. It doesn't mean anything without verse 4. What God is really saying is this: "Are you spending more time with Me…making your heart beautiful…than you are spending on making your body beautiful?" He loves you, and He knows that spending time alone with Him gives you confidence, helps you to know your value in Christ, steers you in the right direction, and gives you internal beauty.

This is our last devotion for SKG, but I hope it won't be your last devotion. Go out and buy another book of devotions. (I actually have one available on my website at secretkeepergirl.com that lasts an entire year!) Or maybe get a journal you can write in every day after you read a Bible verse. Spend time with God each day and see how much more beautiful you become.

In your journal today:

Copy 1 Peter 3:4. Today I want you to write a letter to your dad or mom telling him or her how having devotions has been helpful for you. Ask your parents if they can help you purchase something that will help you keep having devotions.

FAQs

H ello, Secret Keeper Girl moms—

I know you still have lots of questions about your tween daughter, so I've put together the most frequently asked questions we've received on our Secret Keeper Girl website since it debuted in 2004. These seem to be the questions that most often race through moms' minds when they're thinking about modesty and true beauty.

I encourage you to dig deep into God's Word with your daughter to find the answers to all the questions you have, whether I talk about them here or not. And as you dig deeper into the Word together, know that it will reassure her that you do treasure both her and the life God has designed for her.

To get you started, here's a list of the questions I discuss in this section of the book:

- How can I evaluate the modesty of swimwear?
- Can a Christian girl wear the punk-rock look?
- When should a girl start shaving?

- What do you think about the more popular tween magazines out there?

- Is it okay for our daughters to watch TV with older-looking "beauty" icons like Dove Cameron?

- Is there an alternative to the sexy dolls that are popular today?

- Should I be concerned about "sexting" yet, or just when my daughter is older?

- Should a woman wear pants?

- How can you know if your child has been abused?

- When do little girls start hating motherhood?

- Does what I say about my body image affect my tween?

How can I evaluate the modesty of swimwear?

Let me be clear. Swimsuits are not modest. Period. Nothing about them is. My husband and I sat in my home office and struggled with what to say about swimwear because I'm asked so often to address it.

I also want to be truthful and honest about where we are as a family. We do wear swimwear. Let me fill in the picture. We have an old boat that my husband bought for nearly nothing. It had hardly any miles on it. We make up for its years of easy use by using it hard in its retirement years. We ski, jump off cliffs, swim with our labradoodle, and defy death with our eight-foot raft several times each week. Lexi and Autumn, my girls, wear board shorts and T-shirts or tank tops over their suits until they get into the water. Then they change into life preservers, which cover more than T-shirts, and they often keep their shorts on when they get in.

Here are a few tips on how to find modest suits and some guidelines about how to discuss them with your tween or teen daughters:

1. Discuss your expectations *before* **you start looking!** Sit your daughter down and say, "Here are some things I'd like to see you avoid and here are the reasons why." For example, on my list was "no sheer fabric." A quick trip down memory lane to share my "16-year-old-most-embarrassing-moment," which was caused by a wet white one-piece, settled that issue for my girls. (And gave them something to laugh about!)

Also on my list: no bikinis, no low necklines, and no high-cut hips. Discussing these things early lets your daughter know what the guidelines are. One of my teenagers rebutted my annual "no bikini" speech with, "You just don't understand, because no one wore bikinis back when you were a teenager!" I explained that "back in the day," I was often the only girl at a pool party in a one-piece. This drew a response of disbelief that the bikini had actually been invented when I still had ample collagen in my lips!

2. Be positive by focusing on what they can purchase! I like to go online and actually show my daughters some suits I think are modest and they'll like. This sets the standard. They might not pick exactly what I show them, but they have evidence that modest swimwear can be cute. Showing them also helps establish guidelines. It's really important when you are teaching girls about modesty to show them what you can say "yes" to—or all they hear is "no," and that can crush their spirits.

3. Be sure to shop for cover-ups while you're out there. I'm fine with my girls jumping in the ocean or a pool with a swimsuit, but if there are guys around I expect them to cover up when they get out. "Laying out" may be okay with girlfriends, but not when there are guys there. There are so many adorable cover-ups out there that there's no excuse not to find one. My girls prefer a pair of nice board shorts and a T-shirt to a frilly cover-up, but either can serve as modest attire between the pool and home!

Thanks for being sensitive to where I'm at on this. I do realize you may have far more conservative standards, or more lenient ones. It's not easy to speak out publicly on this topic. But I think this conversation is important. There are a lot of Christian girls reaching for bikinis this season, and I'd like to see them reconsider. Maybe what I've just written will help you continue the dialogue in your home.

Can a Christian girl wear the punk-rock look?

Both the punk-rock and the goth looks are huge! Since a Secret Keeper Girl loves Jesus, she represents life. So we vote "no" to darkness and skulls and crossbones. While that rules out goth in general, it doesn't entirely mean you can't get a little punk rock. Instead of all the death and dark colors, try bright pink with a touch of black. Music-themed clothing and jewelry are all the rage these days. Stripes, plaids, and funky buttons or zippers can also add to a look. My daughter Lexi tends to go toward the punk-rock look (and has worn out my dining-room chairs with her riveted belts!). She never compromises on keeping the look full of life. She pairs black jeans with a black-and-white striped T-shirt, then adds a splash of real-life color to it with a hot-pink scarf. Be creative— help your daughter find a way to express herself while still following the guidelines you have established.

When should a girl start shaving?

I was on a national call-in radio show, and a mom called in pretty freaked out because her 14-year-old wanted to shave. Well, it seems like this issue is related to the all-important topic of protecting you daughter's little-girlhood, so let's talk!

First, let me say that my two girls are 16 now, and I *did not* get to pick when they began to shave. Lexi was about 9 when she came to me and asked in a telltale voice, "Mommy, how old do I have to be to shave?" I smiled and responded, "Well, how did it go?" She reveled in letting me feel her freshly shaven legs…with only a few nicks. I began to teach her how to do it safely, and the passion passed in a few weeks and reappeared when she was about 13. Autumn, my adopted daughter, who being Chinese would not have to shave until she's about 90, took it upon herself to begin around age 14.

Your daughter is going to be curious at some point, and that in itself might be a sign that it's time to talk turkey! Second, let me suggest that shaving isn't something that makes them necessarily appear older (which is something that I've talked about a lot because it's dangerous for them), but at a certain point in their lives it does make them appear…well, uh, clean! I think withholding it when it is something they desire may leave them open to being made fun of. I'd err on the side of cleanliness. So what did I tell the woman who called in? I suggested she buy her daughter a razor!

What do you think about the more popular tween magazines out there?

Today's girls are looking to many media to pattern their sense of self, but none more consistently than hard-copy and online magazines such as *Seventeen* and *GL (Girls Life)*. Surveys reveal the startling fact that girls as young as 11 are digging into these teen magazines. And Christian tweens are not absent from this demographic that's transfixed by these magazines. They tend to view them as eagerly as the non-religiously-active population.

Exactly what are they reading? Well, you should look for yourself if your daughter is peeking past the covers. Many have horoscope readings and other articles that reflect cosmic humanism, New Age philosophy, and other alternative spiritualities. One recent article featured a college girl who was so proud of herself for posing nude for a pornographic magazine. What's worse, some of these magazines—such as *Twist* and *Popstar!*—target the tween market specifically. Here are some representative article titles:

- "*Roe v. Wade*: In Danger of Being Turned Down" (*Teen People*)
- "Cast a Love Spell: A Real Teenage Witch Shows You How" (*Seventeen*)

- "Celtic Cross Reading: What the Future Holds" (*Twist*)
- "Joel Madden Strips Down" (*Teen People*)

The results of reading these magazines can be imagined, but one that is actually traceable is the overall damage to the emotions of their readers. Most women or teen girls who read them report feeling depressed about their looks or weight afterward. One Harvard survey, in searching for the impact of today's fashion- and beauty-saturated media culture, found that two-thirds of underweight 12-year-olds consider themselves to be fat. Did you catch that key word? These girls are *underweight*. Shouldn't there be an alternative?

For me, one alternative is *Sisterhood Magazine*, for Christian teen girls. It was founded by Susie Shellenberger, who had previously founded the wildly popular *Brio* magazine for Focus on the Family. The pages are packed with godly advice, modest fashion, and great role models like Mandisa and Toby Mac. I intentionally introduced my daughter Lexi to Susie's work when she was about 10. Even at age 16 she still loved *Sisterhood Magazine*—and though she was tempted, she passed on the other options!

GL (Girl's Life) magazine is a secular magazine that makes an attempt to bridge the gap between girl and teen with their magazine full of true stories about tween girls. However, they still dip into the world of celeb gossip and some trashy fashion trends. There are others, such as *Sports Illustrated for Kids* and *National Geographic Kids,* which can be safer alternatives.

Is it okay for our daughters to watch TV with older-looking "beauty" icons like Dove Cameron?

In 2005, the *Boston Globe* broke news that broke my heart: the prime-time television show most watched by 9- to 12-year-old girls was *Desperate Housewives*! Contrast this with the fact that when I was a tween, girls were watching *CareBears*. Soon after the *Boston Globe* article, an issue of *Family Circle* featured a story entitled, "Fast Times: When did 7 become the new 16?" It mentioned that children were watching programming created for much older audiences.

But what *is* being created specifically for our daughters? Even shows like *Austin & Ally* and *Jessie* feature older actresses. In general the starlets of these shows are teens doing teen things. And in some cases, the content is decidedly more mature. As an example, *Good Luck Charlie* was the first television show created for children that introduced a same-sex couple into its programming. Is this what our little girls should be feasting on? My research tells me "no."

Moms, be careful. How old should your daughter be when she's presented with a role model that's all about hair and makeup? If a girl of eight or nine feasts on that kind of role model, she's going to want to do teen stuff sooner. And that's not good for her. Be age-appropriate with the TV programs you let your daughter view. Why give her role models who wear makeup and have boyfriends if you don't want her to do either of those things yet?

Hannah Montana was coming to a crest when my girls were about 14 years old, and *that* age was when I let them watch it. Not when they were eight. We were able to discuss the actions of Hannah/Miley and decide if they were good, bad, or neutral. We talked about how ridiculous it was to have a double life—and how a teen could possibly have hair and clothing like that! At the age of 14, my girls could enjoy the fiction of it all and separate themselves from it.

But then, Miley went bad. You have to consider carefully how these actresses live off-camera. That matters too. If they are doing concerts or even music videos you don't want your daughter to view, don't give them influence in her life. Instead, turn on something silly like *Psych* or an old Muppets DVD or even *Little House on the Prairie*, which is back in vogue among the tween set.

Is what you're watching with your children instilling positive values or tearing down the value system you're attempting to build? That's what you need to keep in mind as you make media choices.

Is there an alternative to the sexy dolls that are popular today?

It's been estimated that the line of Bratz dolls products exceeded 100 billion dollars in sales in 2008. Do you have a problem with that? I do. One look might be enough to help you understand why. A Bratz doll's bedroom eyes and pouty lips are complemented by her fishnet stockings and belly-baring shirt. As I've often reported at live events and parenting seminars and on the Secret Keeper Girl blog, the American Psychological Association has criticized the dolls for sending an unhealthy message to girls. (Oh, is that an understatement!) "Bratz dolls are marketed in bikinis, sitting in a hot tub, mixing drinks," an APA report said. "Bratz dolls come dressed in sexualized clothing such as miniskirts, fishnet stockings and feather boas."

Psychologists say that even girls who play with more innocent-looking but excessively "beautified" princess dolls tend to initiate a play world that includes seduction to get the prince. Imagine the life skills this teaches a girl! Is it just play? The experts don't think so. "It puts girls on a conveyer belt to sexual activity," says Diane Levin, PhD, of Wheelock College in Boston, author of *So Sexy So Soon: The New Sexualized Childhood and What Parents Can Do to Protect Their Kids.*

So what's a mom to do when her 8-year-old bellows that she doesn't have the "coolest doll on the planet"? Well, I turned to the world of Groovy Girls. My daughter Lexi loved them! They're… well…groovy. These new-millennium rag dolls feature funky colors and eccentric designs. Lexi collected them by the crateful until she was about 11. Best of all, the makers of Groovy Girls actually state that they are on a mission. Their website claims that "our… dolls provide a safe way for young girls to experience fun, fashion-filled doll play while promoting age-appropriate values and attitudes." I vote Groovy Girls all the way. Now, do you have to go with just this brand? No, but my point is there are options—and they're fun and findable! Go find 'em, Mom!

Should I be concerned about "sexting" yet, or just when my daughter is older?

Well, frankly, I hope you'll wait a few years to give your daughter a cell phone. Waiting is good. It builds discipline. My daughters were 13 when they got theirs. I kind of wish I'd waited until they were 16, like I did with my son, Rob. You may have a good reason for your daughter to have one sooner.

Either way, sexting is a good thing for you to get on your radar. In the past year I was devastated to find that two of my teen mentees were caught up in the nasty world of sexting. One of them, a sweet home-schooled Christian girl, actually sent a topless photo of herself to a guy. The other, a pastor's daughter, was graphically propositioned for sex through a text message that ended with, "I know your dad is a pastor, but this is none of his business." As a mom, that should make your blood boil! It does mine.

If you have a teen, don't be naive. The stats are alarming—45 percent of teens say they've sent or received a sexual text message. One in five admits to sending or receiving nude photos. This is *common!* (I loathe to use that word for something so vile.) Let me say it again—don't be naive. My friend Vicki Courtney noted on her blog recently that 50 percent of parents whose teens *are* sexually active believe they are not!

How can you know if your teen or tween is involved in something they shouldn't be…particularly sexting? Talk to them! Ask them. Let them know of the dangers, including the fact that sending or receiving a nude photo of someone who is under 16 is considered a crime of child pornography. There are stiff penalties for this, including jail time (though this is very unlikely for younger teens and tweens). Often just asking questions will help your child feel comfortable to open up with you about what they are feeling pressured to do. If they don't open up to you, or you become suspicious because of an odd reaction, just ask them to let you check the history on their cell phone. You can look together.

What happens if you find that your child is sexting? I'd be radically protective of them. Contact your cell-phone service provider and change their service to exclude the texting feature. If they themselves have been sending "sext" messages, let me suggest something very loving—*take their phone!* Let them re-earn your trust and get the phone back when they have. Seem extreme? Consider this: How meaningful and helpful to good human communication is a text message? I mean, really! (I do know this: It's very bad for your child's grammar.)

Should a woman wear pants?

Let me show you some scripture verses that help us understand what is acceptable for us to wear as women. Many who believe that women should not wear pants point to Deuteronomy 22:5, which reads, "A woman must not wear a man's clothes and a man must not wear women's clothes. The LORD your God hates anyone who does that." This passage simply doesn't mean what some people conclude from it: that women cannot wear pants.

Let me explain why. First of all, keep in mind that this was written during Old Testament times in the Middle East. At that time and place men wore tunics, robes, or dresses just like women did. Second, you must study Scripture in context. This particular verse is believed to be referring to a practice of that place and time of worshipping Venus by having women wear armor and men wear feminine attire. (This view is supported by verse 10 in the same chapter, which warns the people of God not to wear clothes made of interwoven wool and linen, as this was the custom of another group of idol worshippers.) Thus, the main point of these verses is to command the Israelites to avoid doing things that could be associated with the occult.

This passage's best application today is as an appeal to men to appear masculine and women to appear feminine. For instance, the pants and jeans I wear are cut for the female body. The pants and jeans my husband wears are cut for the male body. We'd look ridiculous in each other's clothes. (That said, even women's pants, jeans, or shorts that are too tight, too low, or too short miss the mark of God's call for us to be modest in how we dress, considering our Christian brothers' God-given attraction to our female shape.)

Also, don't be proud in your liberty to wear pants. Anytime I am asked to speak to a group whose church prefers that women wear dresses, I pack dresses. Anytime I represent another speaker or author who prefers that women wear dresses, I go through my closet to select a good wardrobe that honors her and her preference.

Most of the time, I'm more comfortable in pants. But always be testing your fashion choices to make sure you aren't showing off too much of that God-given shape. As much as we sometimes hate to admit it, you *can* find modest fashion options and should go out of your way to do so!

How can you know if your child has been abused?

Child sexual abuse. It's on the hearts of the staff at Pure Freedom because, recently, a precious mom of a five-year-old contacted us for advice on how to help her daughter through this nightmare. Sadly, our ministry receives a lot of these requests for boys and girls of all ages. Fact is, about 15 to 25 percent of adult women and 5 to 15 percent of adult men were sexually abused as children. It's a frightening reality.

How can you know if your child is a victim? Watch for these signs. First, watch for a sudden and unusual interest in sex or sexual things. Second, consider that sleeping problems or nightmares that seem to stem from nowhere could be a symptom. Third, an unusual fear of going to a certain house, school, or class is sometimes a sign that something bad has happened in that place. Fourth, children of abuse often attempt expressions of sexual molestation in artwork or in their actions during play. These things can be evidence that it's time for you to dig a little deeper to see if there's something your child desperately wants to tell you, but doesn't know how.

If you do find there's abuse present, act quickly to get your child into the care of a trained counselor who can help you and your family make good decisions about the best course of action. Each child, each situation, is different, but every child is tender and needs meticulous attention to specific needs.

When do little girls start hating motherhood?

You read that correctly. By the time they're teens, our daughters feel tremendous pressure to *not* value motherhood. In a survey I completed with Nancy Leigh DeMoss in 2008, we found that the majority of teen girls value a career path more than being a mom. A *Christianity Today* survey in the same year found that the majority of Christians felt it was harmful to encourage young girls to be wives and moms. They felt other roles should be esteemed as valuable.

I hope you disagree. I certainly think that being mom to Robby (my Penn State honors student), Lexi (my budding high-school actress), and Autumn (my brave, newly adopted teen) is my greatest role, along with being their dad's wife. I will leave no greater mark in this world than raising them up to be great citizens and lovers of God.

I participated in a sort of think tank with Nancy Leigh DeMoss, Mary Kassian (author of *Girls Gone Wise in a World Gone Wild*), and other key leaders to figure out what we can do to correct the problem. Most of the women at the event were writing books about feminism or speaking out on the biblical view of feminism. I wasn't. I was there mostly to lend my thoughts on how we can engage teen girls in embracing a biblical view of their femininity. Can you guess what my advice is going to be? Don't focus on the teens! Focus on the little girls…ages 8 to 12. As I've pointed out throughout this book, those are the years when values are formed. Those are the years—for the most part—in which we define our concept of marriage, determine our sexual values, make decisions about our life goals, and so on. Sounds so young. But it's true. If you have an 8- to 12-year-old girl, talk to her about how much you love being her mom. Let her know that it's the best thing since sliced bread. And pass on the value of motherhood by valuing her!

Does what I say about my body image affect my tween?

Okay, moms and big sisters. Listen up about the belly fat. (Just to make it clear, I admit I buy my share of New Year's resolution–motivated fitness magazines.)

When I take an honest look and give myself an honest listen, I'm confronted with my own ability to harm my daughters. How can getting fit be harmful to your daughters? Well, it seems that when we say, "I look soooo fat" they internalize it. Unfortunately, it doesn't translate to a thought about *you,* but a thought about *them*! Studies have been done that confirm that what a mom says about her own body becomes a consuming thought in her daughter's mind about *her own* body. The result? One magazine reported that about 30 percent of ten-year-olds are worried about their body image. These are thin, healthy-looking tweens…but between the messages from magazine covers and our own obsession with love handles, they don't have a chance.

God wants you to love how He created *you* as much as you want your daughter to love how He created *her.* That's a habit best *caught,* not *taught*! So go ahead, pull out those dumbbells. Dust off your running shoes. Drink your protein shakes. But keep it positive. It'll help keep your daughter's head straight.

Notes

1. Dennis and Barbara Rainey, *Parenting Today's Adolescent* (Nashville, TN: Nelson, 1998), 5.

2. Becky Freeman, *Mom's Everything Book for Daughters* (Grand Rapids, MI: Zondervan, 2002), 29.

3. Freeman, 30.

4. The Medical Institute for Sexual Health (www.medinstitute.org) "was founded to confront the global epidemics of teen pregnancy and sexually transmitted infections (STIs). We identify and evaluate scientific information on sexual health and promote healthy sexual decisions and behaviors by communicating credible scientific information" (www.medinstitute.org/public/243.cfm).

5. Freeman, 34.

6. Joshua Mann, Joe S. McIlhaney Jr., and Curtis C. Stine, *Building Healthy Futures* (Austin, TX: Medical Institute for Sexual Health, 2000), 21.

7. Josh McDowell, *Why True Love Waits* (Wheaton, IL: Tyndale, 2002), 149.

8. Tim and Beverly LaHaye, *Raising Sexually Pure Kids* (Sisters, OR: Multnomah, 1998), 84.

9. Rainey, 85.

10. James C. Dobson, *Solid Answers* (Wheaton, IL: Tyndale, 1997).

11. Some New Testament passages that address hair include 1 Corinthians 11:14-15; 1 Timothy 2:9; 1 Peter 3:3. Old Testament passages mainly deal with the Nazarite vow, which included not cutting or shaving one's hair, which was believed to be an outward symbol of one's humility and willingness to be used by God. Just prior to coming into the tabernacle, the Nazarite was permitted to shave ceremonially. Such passages include Leviticus 14:8-9; Numbers 6:5; Judges 16:17-22.

Other Resources from Dannah Gresh

Secret Keeper Girl® Series
Six Ways to Keep the "Little" in Your Girl
Guiding Your Daughter from Her Tweens to Her Teens

Today's world pressures girls to act older than they are when they're not ready for it. How can you help your tween daughter navigate the stormy waters of boy-craziness, modesty, body image, media, Internet safety, and more?

Dannah Gresh shares six easy ways to help your daughter grow up to be confident, emotionally healthy, and strong in her faith. In a warm and transparent style, Dannah shows you how to

- help your daughter celebrate her body in a healthy way
- unbrand her when the world tries to buy and sell her
- unplug her from a plugged-in world
- dream with her about her future

Six Ways to Keep the "Good" in Your Boy
Guiding Your Son from His Tweens to His Teens

God created boys to become men who are *good*—embracing God's call to unselfishly provide and protect. As a mom, you have a unique role in this process.

Dannah Gresh blends thorough analysis of the trends that can impact your son—including porn, aggressive girls, and video games gone overboard—with positive, practical advice any mom can use effectively to help guide her son toward "good" during the vital ages of 8 to 12. Dannah shows you

- why a boy needs to play outside
- how reading good books makes him a leader
- what role a mom plays in his entrance into manhood
- tips to keep him unplugged from impurity

----

*With special insights for dads from Bob Gresh
and for single moms from Angela Thomas*

What is a
Secret Keeper Girl?

Well, she's a lot of things. And she's NOT a lot of things. She's NOT a mean girl. She's a girl whose friendships are full of kindness. She's NOT boy crazy. (Moms, can we get an Amen?) She's a girl who knows she can share all of her heart-secrets with her mom at any time.

She's also a girl who embraces modesty. Why? Because she knows that she is a masterpiece created by God. She strives to keep the deepest secrets of her authentic beauty a secret! Maybe you are new to our movement, or maybe you are a long-time Secret Keeper Girl who has been to a live event. Maybe you have already read "Secret Keeper" and been on eight great dates with your Momma! Regardless, you, sweet girl, are a Secret Keeper Girl because you are a masterpiece created by God's hand.

Secret Keeper GIRL
SecretKeeperGirl.com

Like us on Facebook!
Follow us on Twitter!

8 Great Dates for Your Daughter—
with You and with Dad!

Talking with Your Daughter About Best Friends and Mean Girls
Dannah Gresh

One of the best ways to guide your girl toward healthy friendships is to spend quality time with her yourself. The popular 8 Great Dates series from Secret Keeper Girl offers the most fun you'll ever have digging in to God's Word with your daughter. (Think: shopping sprees, slumber parties, ding-dong-ditching, and more!) Eight creative dates help you and your daughter tackle questions like...

- Why do I feel jealous of my BFF sometimes?
- How should I act when I get left out?
- Is it okay to be boy-crazy?

Creative ideas and godly guidance help you bond with your daughter and protect her as she navigates the crazy tween world of friendships using God's truth as her standard.

8 Great Dates for Dads and Daughters
Talking with Your Daughter About Understanding Boys
Bob Gresh and Dannah Gresh

Our culture pressures girls to crush on boys way too soon, but a dad's involvement in his daughter's growing interest is her greatest protection.

Bob and Dannah Gresh have created these 8 Great Dates to help a father and daughter connect on a topic that really matters—and have a terrific time together. (Think: pulling pranks, treasure hunting, and more as you consider God's Word.) You'll tackle big questions from your daughter's point of view...

- What was God thinking when he created girls to like boys?
- Why is everyone boy-crazy? Should I be?
- When can I start to date? (It's not too soon to talk about it!)
- How can I embrace purity?

Here's a simple and complete resource with fresh ways to build your connection with your little girl—and to love and protect her as she grows up.

Also from Harvest House

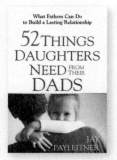

52 Things Daughters Need from Their Dads
What Fathers Can Do to Build a Lasting Relationship
Jay Payleitner

The days of tea parties, stuffed doggies, and butterfly kisses are oh-so-important, but they don't last forever. So how can a dad safeguard his daughter so she grows up strong, healthy, beautiful, and confident? How can you demonstrate your love in a way she'll understand? How can you hold her close and let her go at the same time?

The good news, Dad, is that you are the right man for the job.

Jay Payleitner has given valuable, man-friendly advice to thousands of dads in his bestselling *52 Things Kids Need from a Dad*. Now Jay guides you into what may be unexplored territory—girl land—and gives you ways to...

- date your daughter
- be on the lookout for "hero moments" and make lasting memories
- protect her from eating disorders and other cultural curses
- scare off the scoundrels and welcome the young men who might be worthy
- give your daughter a positive view of men

Jay will help you feel encouraged with 52 creative ideas to give you confidence in relating to your precious daughter...in ways that will help her blossom into the woman God has designed her to be.

To learn more about Harvest House books and
to read sample chapters, visit our website:

www.harvesthousepublishers.com

HARVEST HOUSE PUBLISHERS
EUGENE, OREGON

Just for You, God's Secret Keeper Girl:
Girl Gab Pullouts

Date #1

Your Beauty in God's Eyes

Welcome to SKG. That stands for *Secret Keeper Girl*. What is a Secret Keeper Girl? Think hard and you may remember. Can you fill in this blank?

_____

A Secret Keeper Girl is one who keeps the deepest secrets of her beauty for her future husband. Also, she knows that there aren't any secrets she can't share within the safety of her relationship with her mom. And the coolest thing about a Secret Keeper Girl is that she is a masterpiece created by God.

> *"We are the clay, you are the potter; we*
> *are all the work of your hand."*
> *Isaiah 64:8*

God Himself took the time to carefully craft you into being! You must be a masterpiece!

Value Evaluation

Okay, let's take girl talk to a new level. It's called Girl Gab. So, are you a Styrofoam cup, a ceramic mug, or a priceless piece of china in the following areas? Look over the list and then write an X in the column that best fits you.

	Styrofoam	Ceramic	China
In the way I talk about my dad or husband			
In the way I talk to my mom or daughter			
In the clothes I wear			
In the clothes I want to wear			
In the way I care for and style my hair			
In the way I care for my face each day			
In the way I care for my body and skin			
In the time I spend with God each day			
In the way I treat other people			
In the movies and TV I watch			
In the magazines I read			
The friends I select tend to be…			
My friends tend to pull me toward…			

Now for each area where you selected "Styrofoam" or "Ceramic" for yourself, come up with one specific idea of how you can move toward presenting yourself as a priceless piece of china.

Areas Where I Need to Improve the Way I Present Myself

Okay, how can you improve? If you gave yourself a "Styrofoam" evaluation for the way you've been watching TV, think of something you need to do to change. You might write, "I'm going to try to watch only 30 minutes a day, and only after my homework is done."

Areas Where I Need to Improve

1. . . . .
. . . .
. . . .
. . . .

2. . . . .
. . . .
. . . .
. . . .

3. . . . .
. . . .
. . . .
. . . .

4. . . . .
. . . .
. . . .
. . . .

5. . . . .
. . . .
. . . .
. . . .

 Take some time as mother and daughter to encourage each other in those areas where you want to improve.

Real Physical Beauty

So, Secret Keeper Girl, can you find God's definition of beauty? Dig deep down under all this world's junk and you'll see it. It's nothing like what we imagined it might be. God's Word says this:

> *"Sixty queens there may be and eight*
> *concubines and virgins beyond number;*
> *but my dove, my perfect one, is unique."*
> Song of Songs 6:8-9

Real physical beauty is those special things about you that are unlike anyone else. Kind of funny, isn't it? Those are sometimes the things that make us feel most uncomfortable because they're...well, different. But God says that's what makes us beautiful. I want you to look at yourself piece by piece today. Can you see that unique beauty?

My Unique Beauty

Complete the sentences below. Then, talk about it as mom and daughter.

My hair is_____

My eyes are _____

My nose is _____

My teeth are_____

My face is_____

My complexion is _____

My smile is _____

My weight is _____

My height is_____

My chest is_____

My legs are _____

My hands are _____

The most unique physical trait about me is _____

_____

Okay, let's be real. We all have things about us that make us feel more bashful than beautiful. What's yours?

. . . .
. . . .
. . . .
. . . .
. . . .
. . . .
. . . .
. . . .
. . . .
. . . .
. . . .

Guess what? God has got that covered! Second Corinthians 1:4 says,

*"Praise be to the God of all comfort
who comforts us in all our troubles
so we can comfort others!"*

Some people might try to tell you that braces or zits are no big deal. But they are! Anything that makes you feel bad is a big deal. Just don't forget that God wants to comfort you. And He just might use you to help the dozens of other friends around you who feel the exact same way about the exact same thing!

Doodle Box

The Source of Beauty

Where does beauty really come from? As girls we sometimes get stuck on thinking it comes from a great haircut or a totally awesome new fingernail polish. Sometimes we think it comes from being surrounded by beautiful friends or being noticed by cute guys. But these are dry streams. You won't find beauty there.

> *"Your beauty should not come from outward adornment, such as braided hair and the wearing of gold jewelry and clothes. Instead, it should be that of your inner self, the unfading beauty of a gentle and quiet spirit, which is of great worth in God's sight."*
> 1 Peter 3:3-4

The source of true beauty is the presence of God!

The Absolute Beauty Challenge

How 1 Peter 3:3-4 is really challenging you could be said like this: "Do you spend more time in front of the mirror making yourself beautiful on the outside, or do you spend more time developing your inner beauty through spending quiet time with God?"

Here's a fun way to change. Take my Absolute Beauty Challenge (A-B-C). Here's how it works:

> **A.** Challenge yourself each day to spend a little more time with God than you spend working on your hair, face, clothing, and so on. Don't worry too much about watching the clock, but do try to push yourself—it will change you a lot. Maybe you take about 15 minutes to get ready each morning—you can set a goal of spending 15 or 20 minutes a day with God (and Mom will help because she'll be doing it too!). I want you to do this for the next four weeks, for five out of seven days each week. And to make it really fun, put something on the line in case you miss a day. For example, you might say that if you miss, you'll clean your mom's shoe closet the next week. If she misses, she might have to clean your hamster cage!

B. Agree to the challenge by signing the Absolute Beauty Challenge. When you get home, get a copy to tape to your bathroom mirror.

C. Every day, read the verse on the challenge and ask yourself the question, "Today, did I spend more time in God's Word or in front of this mirror?"

Are you ready to dive in? If so, sign the Absolute Beauty Challenge. Post it in your bedroom or bathroom where you can see it every day when you're getting ready.

Doodle Box

Absolute Beauty Challenge
(It's as easy as A-B-C.)

*"Your beauty should not come from outward adornment,
such as braided hair and the wearing of gold jewelry
and clothes. Instead, it should be that of your inner self,
the unfading beauty of a gentle and quiet spirit
which is of great worth in God's sight."*
1 Peter 3:3-4

**"Today, did I spend more time in
God's Word or in front of the mirror?"**

We, _____ and _____, will
attempt to spend _____ and _____ minutes a
day in quiet prayer and Bible reading during the next
four weeks. We commit to doing this for five out of every
seven days. If one of us misses more than two days in a
week, that person will _____ for the other.

(Ideas of things you can do for each other if you miss
more than two days include cleaning out the other person's closet out, giving them a foot rub and manicure,
walking the dog when it's their turn, or doing the dishes
while the other one relaxes!)

Signed: _____

Date: _____

To make it easier to have devotions, *8 Great Dates for
Moms and Daughters* includes 20 mini-devotions. See
page 115.

The Power of Beauty

God created your beauty with a special power. The Bible calls it the power to intoxicate. But it's for just one man...your future husband. Remember, a Secret Keeper Girl is one who saves the deepest secrets of her beauty for just one man. Each and every day the clothes you choose to wear are a part of saving the deepest secrets of your beauty for just him!

> *"May your fountain be blessed and may you rejoice*
> *in the wife of your youth. A loving doe, a graceful*
> *deer...May you ever be captivated by her love."*
> Proverbs 5:18-19

God created you with an intoxicating power called beauty, and it is your responsibility to handle it with care.

A Doodling Lesson

Check out this little graphic.

What do you see? You probably see a man.

Is he happy or sad? You might even guess that he's happy.

Hmm! I show you a couple of curved lines and a circle, and you see a happy little guy! What is up with that? That's the Gestalt theory at work. The Gestalt theory teaches an artist to control a viewer's time and attention by forcing the person to mentally complete a visual image. Because the brain is intrigued by completing the incomplete, it will always pause to finish an unfinished picture.

Check out this trio of circles.

What else do you see? (Answer: A triangle)

Can you draw a bird using the Gestalt theory? How about a mountain?

I'm not just telling you this for no reason. It has a lot to do with the power of your beauty. How? Well, what does a guy see when a girl walks by him wearing a tiny little pair of low-rider shorts and a belly shirt? Write your answer below:

. . . .
. . . .
. . . .

How about when a girl wears a long, tight skirt with a slit all the way up the sides?

. . . .
. . . .
. . . .

Are there any clothes you wear that invite someone to finish the picture?

. . . .
. . . .
. . . .

What can you do to avoid wearing clothes that invite people to finish the picture of your body?

. . . .
. . . .
. . . .

Your drawings here!

Truth or Bare Fashion

In the '80s, when I was a teen, socks were huge! We had three pairs of socks to match each outfit, and we wore them all at the same time! We even had something called leg warmers, which were huge, fuzzy socks to wear over our jeans all the way up to our knees! Trends come. Trends go. Does God care about them? Fashion trends are not His biggest concern, but I think He does care. He certainly doesn't want us to just follow the crowd!

> *"Do everything without complaining or arguing so that*
> *you may become blameless and pure, children of God*
> *without fault in a crooked and depraved generation,*
> *in which you shine like stars in the universe."*
> *Philippians 2:14-15*

God's Word doesn't diss fashion. But it calls us to be careful in the way we express our beauty. If we obey Him, we'll probably stand out a little. That's a good thing. But we're always called to share our beauty cautiously!

Today's Hot Looks!

Okay, let's test all the current fashion trends against God's Word. First, read all the different fashion trends I've listed in the left column on the next page. Go ahead and add any that you think I've missed. Include specific things you've had your eye on, like a certain style of shirt or a pair of sneakers.

Now in the column labeled "How I see them," write down the main characteristics or things people wear when they're trying to get that look.

Today's hot looks	How I see them	Pass, fail, or use caution
The beach look	Suit, cover-ups, bikini	Bikinis fail. Use caution with a cover-up.
The prom look		
Miniskirts		
The cowgirl look		
Grunge		
Goth		
Preppy		
Punk		
Athletic		
The '50s look		
Designer labels		
Belly rings		
Tattoos		

Now you can decide if these looks *pass, fail,* or deserve *caution* based on a few Bible verses I think help us evaluate fashion. (Some of these will be familiar to you.)

Is this look feminine?

*"A woman must not wear men's clothing, nor
a man wear women's clothing, for the LORD
your God detests anyone who does this."*
Deuteronomy 22:5

God wants you to look like a girl…not a guy. That doesn't mean you can't wear pants. It just means you shouldn't wear pants that are cut for men or anything else that is considered manly in our society. Are there any things in the chart that you feel God wouldn't want you to wear because they don't let you look like a girl?

Does this look hide my "intoxicating" secrets?

*"Rejoice in the wife of your youth. A loving doe, a graceful
deer…May you ever be captivated by her love."*
Proverbs 5:18-19

God wants you to save the deepest secrets of your beauty… your breasts, your belly skin, your thighs, and your bottom…for just one man. Does this trend make you look fabulous without drawing attention to these parts of your body?

Is this look joyful?

"Be joyful always."
1 Thessalonians 5:16

God wants you to look like a girl who worships Him. Since worshipping Him fills us with joy, we need to make sure we don't clothe ourselves in dark and dreary attire. Are there any looks above that you should avoid for that reason?

Is it affordable?

> *"Your beauty should not come from outward adornment,*
> *such as braided hair and the wearing of gold jewelry*
> *and fine clothes. Instead, it should be that of your*
> *inner self, the unfading beauty of a gentle and quiet*
> *spirit, which is of great worth in God's sight."*
> *1 Peter 3:3-4*

God doesn't want you to be consumed with how much you spent on an outfit or whether it's a certain brand. It doesn't mean we can't have a certain brand if it's comfortable and affordable, but we shouldn't whine for things we can't afford. Are there any things above that need to be disqualified for this reason?

Does it honor my parents?

> *"Honor your father and your mother, so*
> *that you may live long in the land."*
> Exodus 20:12

A Secret Keeper Girl can't wear anything her parents don't want her to wear, and she has to obey their preferences with honor. So, do you need to cross anything off for this reason?

Do I really like it, or do I just think my friends will like it?

> *"Am I now trying to win the approval of men,*
> *or of God?...If I were still trying to please*
> *men, I would not be a servant of Christ."*
> Galatians 1:10

It's okay to want something because you think it's neat, but watch out when you start buying things just because your friends have them.

Doodle Box

The Bod Squad

W ell, here you are with your special friends, otherwise known as The Bod Squad! Friends can offer good peer pressure to help you make modest choices in the years ahead. Remember, peer pressure is when your friends or acquaintances influence you to do what is right or what is wrong. Do you remember what I said about peer pressure and fashion on the CD?

"He who walks with the wise grows wise."
Proverbs 13:20

For today, it might as well read, "She who shops with wise friends will wear great fashion!"

Truth or Bare Fashion Tests!

Before we set you loose to shop, I have a few modesty tests every single outfit has to pass. I like to call them the SKG Truth or Bare Fashion Tests. Review each test and take them as a group.

Test: Raise & Praise

Target question: **Am I showing too much belly?**

Action: **Stand straight up and pretend you are going for it in worship. Extend your arms in the air to God. Is this exposing a lot of belly? Bellies are very intoxicating, and we need to save that intoxication for our husband!**

Remedy: Go to the guys' department and buy a simple ribbed T-shirt (otherwise known as a Secret Keeper Girl Secret Weapon) to wear under your funky short T's or with your trendy low-riders. Layers are also a great solution to belly shirts.

Test: Grandpa's Mirror

Target question: **How short is too short?**

Action: **Get in front of a full-length mirror. If you're in shorts, sit crisscross applesauce. If you're in a skirt, sit in a chair with your legs crossed. Now, what do you see in that mirror?**

Okay, pretend it's your grandpa! If you see undies, or lots of thigh, your shorts or skirt is too short.

ReMedy: Buy longer shorts and skirts!

✿ Test: I See London, I See France

Target question: **Can you see my underpants?**

Action: **Bend over and touch your knees. Have a friend look right at your bottom. Can she see the outline of your underpants or the seams in them? How about the color of them? Can she see your underwear itself because your pants are so low that you're risking a "plumber" exposure? If so, you bomb on this test.**

ReMedy: Wear white panties with white clothes. If your pants are so tight that you can see the outline of your panties, try buying one size larger.

✿ Test: Spring Valley

Target question: **"Is my shirt too tight?"**

Action: **You probably aren't quite ready for this test, so we'll have the moms take it! Have them place the tips of their fingers together and press into their shirts right in the "valley" between the breasts. Count to three and have them take their fingers away. If their shirts spring**

back like a mini-trampoline, they're too tight. Even though this might not be a problem for you just yet, it won't be long until you'll need to be careful about wearing shirts that are too tight.

Remedy: **Don't buy clothes based on size. Buy them based on fit. Usually, you have to go a few sizes larger these days to have a modest fit.**

❀ Test: Over & Out

Target question: **"Is my shirt too low?"**

Action: **Lean forward a little bit. Can you see too much chest skin or future cleavage? If so, your shirt is too low.**

Remedy: **Today's fashions thrive on low shirts. Layering them is often the only remedy. Throw a little T-shirt under a rugby, and you have a great look.**

Is My Swimsuit Modest?

Oh, girlfriend! That is a hard question. I would say that your swimsuit needs to pass nearly all of these tests. Can you raise and praise without showing off your belly? Can you bend over without showing off cleavage? Can you sit with your legs crisscrossed and look in a mirror without your suit gapping at the crotch? And still…swimsuits aren't high on the modesty scale unless you're in the water! So when you jump out, don't flaunt your body—instead, cover up with a simple pair of shorts and a T-shirt or one of the cute little cover-ups available today!

Date #7

Internal Fashion

Ever meet a girl who just looked so cool but then turned out to be a snob? Notice how her beauty fades? Of course, maybe you've also met a girl who at first glance doesn't seem that beautiful, but the more you're around her, the more fabulous she looks to you. That's internal beauty you're seeing. A Secret Keeper Girl isn't complete without fashion for her heart.

> *"Man did not come from woman, but woman from man;*
> *neither was man created for woman, but woman for*
> *man. For this reason, and because of the angels, the*
> *woman ought to have a sign of authority on her head."*
> *1 Corinthians 11:8-10*

Women in Bible days were so committed to the internal fashion of submission that they wore their hair a certain way—or had some kind of hat on—as an external reminder for themselves and everyone else around them. Wow! Don't you think it'd be cool if our culture cared so much about how we looked on the inside that we wore a symbol of it on the outside? We don't do that anymore, and I don't think it's necessary, but I do like the idea that both men and women understood the idea of mutual respect and submission.

Fashion for My Heart

Clothes aren't the only things we wear. God invites us to "wear" things on the inside too. Check out these verses and discover some of the hottest fashions for the heart. Underline the things we're called to "wear."

"[A woman of God] is clothed
with strength and dignity."
Proverbs 31:25

"Put on the full armor of God...Stand firm then, with
the belt of truth buckled around your waist, with the
breastplate of righteousness in place, and with your
feet fitted with the readiness that comes from the
gospel of peace. In addition to all this, take the shield
of faith, with which you can extinguish all the flaming
arrows of the evil one. Take the helmet of salvation and
the sword of the Spirit, which is the word of God."
Ephesians 6:13-17

"I...want women to dress modestly, with decency...with good deeds appropriate for women who profess to worship God."
1 Timothy 2:9-10

"Your beauty should not come from outward adornment...[but from] a gentle and quiet spirit."
1 Peter 3:3-4

The things you've underlined are all vital parts of a Secret Keeper Girl's wardrobe. The most vital internal garment for you is submission. Submission is allowing someone else to lead you. Submitting doesn't require you to mindlessly follow a bad example. Submission invites you to sometimes let a good friend get to play the game she wants to play even if you'd rather not. Submission requires you to qui-etly honor your parents, teachers, and other authorities with obedi-ence. What a privilege! (What a tough task!) So how do you know if you're wearing it? It's not like you can see it. Let's see if you've got submission hanging in your internal power ward-robe.

Submission Scale Quiz

Circle the statement that sounds most like you.

1. When the kids I'm hanging with decide they want to do something I don't want to do, I
   a. yell and grumble and run home stomping all the way
   b. keep talking until I convince everyone to do what I want to do
   c. try to listen to everyone's feelings and help all of us work it out—even though this is hard to do
   d. do what my friends prefer—after all, everyone deserves a turn to lead

2. When the teacher gives me homework, I usually
   a. refuse to do it
   b. do it, but the whole time I think it's dumb because I already know it all
   c. wish I didn't have to, but I don't want to disappoint my teacher
   d. do it without thinking too much—after all, she's the teacher!

3. When my parents ask me to do something, I
   a. throw a royal fit and ask to be paid
   b. grumble and do it half right
   c. feel sad because I'm not getting to do what I want, but I get it done
   d. do it with all my heart because I want to please my parents

4. When my brother or sister wants the same video game or toy that I want, I

> **a.** tease him or her the whole time as I play with the toy
> **b.** tell him what I think he should be doing
> **c.** ask if I can have it first, and let the other person wait for his or her turn
> **d.** let the other person go first and find something else to do

5. When I think someone has made a mistake, I

> **a.** want to be the first to correct the person, and I do it as loudly as possible
> **b.** try to take over because I can do it better
> **c.** watch for a good time to bring it up quietly
> **d.** wait for adults or others in authority to make things right

6. I go to church because

> **a.** my parents make me, but I wouldn't if I could help it
> **b.** I have to, but I never really learn anything
> **c.** I have good friends there
> **d.** I want to be what God wants me to be, and church is a great place to learn this

So, how'd ya do? Count up all your a's, b's, c's, and d's.
Write the totals below.

_____ A _____ B _____ C _____ D

Which letter did you have the most of? Circle that letter below to find out how you're doing.

D. Submissive Servant
Wow! I wish I could score this high. Keep up the great work. Just don't let it go to your head.

C. Sensitive Socialite
Good eye, girlfriend. You recognize your own desires, but you're trying hard to put others ahead of yourself, and you often succeed.

B. Boisterous Boss
Try harder! You probably have a lot of leadership potential, but God can't use that until you learn some gentleness. Work on controlling your tongue.

A. Raging Rebel
Uh-oh! Watch out! You're wearing the wrong stuff, girl. You need to work on controlling your tongue and your emotions.

Date #8

Box of Questions for Date #8: Affirmation of Beauty

Dad: "God carefully and precisely created your daughter to be beautiful. Describe the first moment you saw her."

Dad: "Your daughter has been learning that internal beauty is more important than external beauty. What's the most beautiful thing about her heart?"

Dad: "Your daughter has been learning that her body has the power to intoxicate guys. Tell her your perspective as a dad on how a guy thinks about girls."

Dad: "Beauty is the unique features about us that no one else has. What unique feature or features about your wife attracted you to her?"

Mom: "How did you tell your daughter's dad that you were pregnant with her?"

Mom: "What part of your daughter's face most looks like you? What part most looks like her dad?"

Mom: "What's your daughter's favorite book?"

Daughter: "What's the most fun you've ever had with your dad? Why?"

Daughter: "When do you most sense your dad's love? Is it a) when he hugs you or b) when he does things with you? Why?"

Daughter: "Fill in the blank. 'My beauty is ultimately determined by _____.'"

Daughter: "Tell your dad about the effect of the Gestalt theory. (Possible answer: "The human brain craves the completion of an incomplete image, so although sometimes we can see only a couple of curvy lines and a dot, our minds create the image of a person.") How does this relate to fashion?"

Daughter: "Tell your mom and dad which SKG date was your favorite and why."

Daughter: "Name three internal fashions we should wear." (Possible answers: submission, good deeds, a gentle spirit, truth, strength, dignity, and so on.)